Schaum's Quick Guide to Writing Great Essays

D0982166

Forthcoming titles:

Schaum's Quick Guide to Writing Great Essays

Molly McClain
Jacqueline D. Roth

McGraw-Hill

New York   San Francisco   Washington, D.C.   Auckland   Bogotá
Caracas   Lisbon   London   Madrid   Mexico City   Milan
Montreal   New Delhi   San Juan   Singapore
Sydney   Tokyo   Toronto

Library of Congress Catalog Card Number: 98-067035

McGraw-Hill

A Division of The **McGraw·Hill** Companies

13 14 DOC/DOC 0

ISBN 0-07-047170-3

The sponsoring editor for this book was Barbara Gilson, the editing supervisor was Fred Dahl, the designer was Inkwell Publishing Services, and the production supervisor was Tina Cameron. It was set in New Century Schoolbook by Inkwell Publishing Services.

Printed and bound by R. R. Donnelley & Sons Company.

McGraw-Hill books are available at special quantity discounts to use as premiums and sales promotions, or for use in corporate training sessions. For more information, please write to the Director of Special Sales, McGraw-Hill, Professional Publishing, Two Penn Plaza, New York, NY 10121-2298. Or contact your local bookstore.

Contents

Preface

Schaum's Quick Guide to Writing Great Essays is concerned with only one type of writing: the essay. If you are in college, knowing how to write an essay is a practical matter of survival, for it is the basis of essay exams as well as student research papers. Even the most simple assignments—those asking you to summarize and comment on a text—depend on your ability to understand the structure of an author's argument.

Once you are out of college, you will find that the essay is the basis of nonfiction books, newspaper and magazine articles, speeches, legal briefs and opinions, and persuasive business communications. Regardless of what profession you choose to enter, you are going to be called on to use the principles you learned in writing the essay to present your ideas to others.

If you need detailed help in other areas of writing, such as writing as an expressive art form, there are some excellent books available at your local bookstore.

MOLLY MCCLAIN
JACQUELINE D. ROTH

Schaum's Quick Guide to Writing Great Essays

Part I

MAKE AN ARGUMENT

An essay is assigned to enable a student to learn three things:

1. **How to explore a subject area and to make a judgment about a particular issue.**
2. How to create an argument supporting that judgment using reasoning and evidence.
3. How to write an interesting and coherently organized essay.

The purpose of writing an essay is to persuade an educated, and critical, reader that your point of view on a topic is correct. You cannot do this by indulging in emotional pleas or by listing fact after innumerable fact. Instead, you must make a well-reasoned and coherent argument that is backed by authoritative evidence. The following chapters will teach you how to do this.

The first section of this book focuses on the development of a *thesis statement,* a declarative sentence that tells your reader what you think about a topic. In other words, it is your opinion. It is also a response to what we have called the *topic question.*

If you are in school, your teachers often will present you with a topic question in the form of an "essay question." Your job is to answer that query and to organize an argument using the available sources. In this case, you may turn directly to Chapter 3, "How to Write a Thesis Statement." However, if you are writing a research paper in which you have to determine your own topic question, read Chapters 1 and 2.

Chapter 1 shows you how to explore a subject area and to find a topic that interests you. This is the first step in writing a research paper, and it is not as easy as it seems. You need to break down a large *subject area* into a smaller number of *topics,* which can be explored in the time and space available. You also need to ask questions—lots of questions—about your topic. This will help you to focus your thinking and to find an important question to write about.

Chapter 2 shows you how to identify the *topic question* that will direct your research and lead directly to your thesis statement. This is the most important, and often the most neglected, feature of essay writing. If you do not have a topic question, you will not be able to formulate a thesis statement.

Chapter 3 shows you how to turn your topic question into a clear and forceful thesis statement. It also provides you with ways to evaluate your thesis. Have you stated it fairly? Can you prove it in the time and space available?

Chapter 1

How to Identify a Topic That Interests You

How do you find a topic—a good topic—for your essay? You start by defining the larger *subject* about which you are required to write. For example, if you are taking a class on the history of China, you may choose to write an essay on the subject of "China in Revolution." Of course, you cannot describe the whole history of Communist China in a ten-page research paper. Instead, you have to break this general subject down into smaller, more manageable *topics*. Once you select several possible topics, you use the reasoning process called *inquiry* to explore those topics further.

This chapter shows you how to find a topic that can be explored in the amount of time available and with the research materials on hand. It also lists some questions that you need to ask at this stage of the research process. It is crucial for you to ask many questions about the topics you are exploring. Questions help you to refine your thinking and to formulate a good *topic question;* they also shape the direction of your research.

Finally, we encourage you to ask *so what?* Why do you think that your topic is important and relevant? How can you draw on your own special interests, experiences, and abilities to write an interesting and intellectually stimulating essay? If you take the trouble to find a topic about which you care deeply, you are likely to write a very good essay. If you are bored by your topic—trust us—your readers will be too.

I. What Are Subjects and Topics?

A. WHAT IS A SUBJECT?

1. A *subject* is the area of knowledge where you will search for a topic and a topic question. Think of the subject as a large box filled with smaller boxes of the same size and shape.

2. The name of your college class can serve as your subject.

EXAMPLES:

History of China (History)

Principles of Broadcast Communication (Communication Studies)

Christianity and Its Practice (Theological and Religious Studies)

B. WHAT IS A TOPIC?

1. A *topic* is a category within a subject. If you think of the subject as a large box filled with smaller boxes, then the topic is one of those smaller boxes.

2. Each topic is composed of more narrow *subtopics,* which, in turn, can be broken down into smaller units.

EXAMPLE 1:

    a. SUBJECT: History of China (History)

        (1) TOPIC: China in Revolution

            A. SUBTOPIC: Economic Reform

                1. NARROWER SUBTOPIC: Mao Tse-tung's Five-Year Plan

EXAMPLE 2:

    b. SUBJECT: Principles of Broadcast Communication (Communication Studies)

        (1) TOPIC: Radio

            B. SUBTOPIC: Ethnic Radio Broadcasting

                1. NARROWER SUBTOPIC: WDIA Radio Station, Memphis, TN, the First Afro-American Radio Station

    c. SUBJECT: Christianity and Its Practice (Theological and Religious Studies)

        (1) TOPIC: Christian Education

            C. SUBTOPIC: Religion in Public Schools

                1. NARROWER SUBTOPIC: School Prayer

C. WHY IS IT IMPORTANT TO MAKE A DISTINCTION BETWEEN A *SUBJECT* AND A *TOPIC*?

By distinguishing between a subject and a topic, you find a preliminary way to organize your research so that you do not get overwhelmed by too much information.

D. HOW DO YOU FIND SUBJECTS AND TOPICS?

Start by looking through *The Library of Congress Subject Headings* (4 vols.) for words, ideas, and/or names of subjects that you find interesting. Each subject is broken down into narrower topics. Related topics and broader subjects are also mentioned. When you search for these subjects in your local library, you need to use the same descriptions used by the Library of Congress.

II. How Do You Identify a "Good" Topic?

A. A GOOD TOPIC FITS WITHIN THE *BOUNDARIES* OF YOUR SUBJECT.

EXAMPLE:

SUBJECT: China in Revolution

    GOOD TOPIC: Mao Tse-tung's Five-Year Plan

    UNRELATED TOPIC: Blue-and-White Porcelain Exports

B. A GOOD TOPIC IS NEITHER *TOO GENERAL* NOR *TOO SPECIFIC.*

    1. A general topic can look boring or unmanageable unless it is narrowed or related to a more specific topic.

EXAMPLE:

TOO GENERAL TOPIC: Artificial Satellites

TOPIC NARROWED: The Involvement of the United Nations in the Regulation of Direct Broadcasting from Satellites

2. A specific topic can look unimportant or difficult to research unless it is related to a more general subject.

EXAMPLE:

TOO SPECIFIC TOPIC: Blue Dog Lake Camp, South Dakota

TOPIC BROADENED: Church Camps as a Form of Outdoor Christian Education

C. A GOOD TOPIC CAN BE HANDLED WITH THE RESEARCH TOOLS YOU HAVE AVAILABLE.

Make sure that you have access to the necessary library resources, archives, and/or lab materials. See Appendix A for research tips. Also, be sure that a faculty member or other professional can give you advice regarding your topic.

D. A GOOD TOPIC CAN BE HANDLED IN THE AMOUNT OF TIME AVAILABLE.

Estimate the amount of time that it will take you to research and write your essay, and choose your topic accordingly. It often takes twice as long to write an essay as it does to research one, a fact that students often forget. Use the following tips to organize your time:

    a. It can take up to two hours to write one page (250 words). This means that a six-page paper can take at least 12 hours to write.

        (1) You are able to write effectively for only six hours per day. So plan to write a six-page paper over the course of two days.

    b. You should spend approximately twice as much time writing a paper as you spend researching one. This means that, if you are writing a six-page paper, you should spend no more than six hours doing preliminary research.

    c. Plan the amount of time that you will need for research and writing. Remember, it is always better to overestimate the amount of time that a job will take than to underestimate it:

Length of Paper (pages)	Research Time (hours)	Writing Time (hours)	Total Time (hours)
3	3	6	9
6	6	12	18
12	12	24	36
24	24	48	72

E. A GOOD TOPIC IS ONE THAT INTERESTS YOU.

Since you are going to spend a good deal of time researching your topic, be sure you are interested in it. If you get bored, so will your readers.

III. How Do You Find a Topic That Interests You?

A. GET AN OVERVIEW OF YOUR SUBJECT BY DOING SOME GENERAL READING.

See Appendix A for research tips.

1. Read the entry on your subject in one of the standard encyclopedias.

2. Skim a review text on your subject and note the relevant chapter and section headings. For example, a review text such as *World History* provides summary information on events such as "Imperialism and Colonial Nationalism" or "World Wars and Dictatorships" in an easy-to-read format.

3. Look at the titles of books on your subject; they may suggest directions for research.

B. MAKE SURE THAT YOU UNDERSTAND "THE BIG PICTURE" FROM YOUR GENERAL READING.

The more you learn about your subject, the easier it is to get bogged down in detail and to overlook the obvious.

1. To keep this from happening, ask yourself two "big picture questions":

a. What does "everyone" know about this subject? In other words, what do people who are knowledgeable, but not necessarily expert, know about your subject?

b. Why is it important to talk about this subject? What makes it particularly relevant at this particular time?

C. ASK "BIG QUESTIONS" ABOUT YOUR SUBJECT.

You will not be able to find all the answers to the big questions during your general reading. Do not worry. At this point, *asking* the questions is far more important than finding the answers. The big questions are:

1. **Who?** Who did it? Who did not do it? Who was it done to? Who else was involved? Who was affected positively or negatively? Who had the most to gain or lose?

2. **What?** What happened? What was the result? What advantage was sought, gained, or lost? What can we learn from this? What was said about it? What does it remind you of? What factors caused this to occur?

3. **When?** When did it happen? When did it begin? When did it end? When did people start to find out about it? When did they begin to do something about it?

4. **Where?** Where did it happen? Where was it most successful? Where was it least successful?

5. **Why?** Why did a given event take place? Why did it become so influential? Why was it ignored? Why did a person or a group get involved? Why did they fail to get involved?

   a. The question *why* can refer to motive, process, or causation.

      (1) When it refers to motive, the question is, "What motivated a person or group to act as they did?"

      (2) When referring to process, it is, "How did an event come to take place?" Or, "what steps can be taken to repeat this event?"

      (3) When referring to causation, it is, "What factors combined to cause an event?" Or, "what was the most important factor to cause an event?"

6. **How?** How did it happen? How did the events unfold? How did an event affect a given person, place, or situation? How did people respond?

7. **How much?** How much did it cost? How high was the cost in political, moral, ethical, religious, or human terms? Do you think that the price paid was too much? How much will it cost in the future?

IV. Identify the "Hot Topics" in Your Subject Area

A. WHY IS THIS IMPORTANT?

You need to know if a new and exciting idea or approach has generated interest in a topic. By becoming aware of new trends in scholarship, you can find interesting topics and avoid duds.

B. WHERE SHOULD YOU LOOK FOR A "HOT TOPIC"?

Scan newspapers and magazines for topics that seem to have caught the attention of an educated readership. Read through the tables of contents of academic journals, and scan popular magazines. Also, look at book reviews published in *The New York Times Review of Books* and in other national publications; reviewers often provide a great deal of information on new trends in scholarship.

C. WHAT SHOULD YOU LOOK FOR?

1. Look for *controversy*. Every author is taking a stand for or against something. The author might be involved in an ongoing controversy or breaking new ground. Try to figure out what is going on.

2. Look for catchwords or clichés. Are people repeating old arguments, old problems, or old solutions without re-examining the facts?

3. Look for topics that have not been fully explored in the material you have read.

V. Identify the Authorities on Your Subject

A. WHAT IS AN AUTHORITY?

An *authority* is an expert who has been recognized by other members of his/her discipline as particularly knowledgeable about a subject. An authority may be a journalist, a freelance writer, a teacher, a faculty member at a college or university, a civil servant, or a scientist. You may never have heard their names, but authorities are well known to other members of their professions.

B. WHY IS IT IMPORTANT TO KNOW WHO THE AUTHORITIES ARE?

If you think of scholarship as a game, then authorities are the key players. Their ideas, books, and articles help to define the "state of play" in a field at any given time. If you are new to the game, as most college students are, it is important for you to find out who the authorities are and what they have written. It is likely that many of the books you read respond to arguments made by one of the authorities in the field. You too might want to join this game by questioning or defending the ideas of one of the leading "players." Or you might want to change the "state of play" by asking different questions altogether.

C. HOW DO YOU FIND THE AUTHORITIES ON YOUR SUBJECT?

1. The best thing to do is to *ask* your instructor or a knowledgeable professional. The world of ideas may seem very large but it is, in reality, a relatively small place. Most college and university teachers and other professionals know the names of the authorities in their disciplines, even if they do not keep up with the "state of play."

2. You might also find and follow a trail of *references*. All scholars refer to the work of others in their footnotes and bibliographies. By looking through these sections, you can find references to authorities on a given subject. A recently published work will contain the most up-to-date references.

3. Be sure to ask your instructor to check your list of authorities. Have you missed anyone important? Is there anyone on your list whose theories are considered outdated or unsound?

VI. Think About What You Have Done So Far

Once you have gained a general knowledge of your subject, ask yourself the following questions and propose some possible answers. Do not censor yourself.

A. HOW DO YOU FEEL ABOUT WHAT YOU HAVE READ?

What is your "gut" response?

1. Which topics are *least* interesting to you?
2. Which topics are you curious about?

B. WHAT DOES NOT ADD UP?

Is something missing? Is something wrong? Is someone not telling the whole story as you know it? Is someone overlooking something, either deliberately or inadvertently?

C. ARE YOUR SYMPATHIES OR FEARS BEING MANIPULATED?

How? Do you resent it? Why? Who is doing the manipulation? What is the reason for doing so? Does the other side deserve to be heard?

D. DO YOU AGREE/DISAGREE WITH THE "AUTHORITIES"?

Why? Do you think that they are missing the point in some way? In what way?

1. Not all knowledge has been found. Your questions and ideas are important and worthwhile. Follow up on them. You may turn out to be the "authority" of the next generation.

E. DO YOU APPROVE/DISAPPROVE OF THE GENERAL INTER-PRETATION? WHY?

F. HOW MUCH OF WHAT YOU HAVE READ APPEARS TO BE CONDITIONED BY ATTITUDES AND ASSUMPTIONS OF AN EARLIER TIME?

1. All authors are influenced by the prevailing attitudes and assumptions of their time, even if they claim to approach their subject "objectively." There is nothing wrong with this. But it does mean that even the best work can look "dated" or old-fashioned when viewed by a younger generation of scholars.

EXAMPLES

Marxist interpretations of history

Freudian interpretations of human psychology

Creationists and Evolutionists on the origin of man

2. As a representative of a younger generation, ask yourself:
   a. Has anything changed since this work was written? Have attitudes changed? Have values changed? Has power shifted? Has new knowledge changed peoples' perceptions?
   b. Is the political situation that produced this set of values still in existence?
   c. What were the ideals then? What are they now?

G. SHOULD THERE BE A CHANGE IN THE CURRENT STATE OF AFFAIRS?

1. Will that change affect you and the group to which you belong?
2. Whose interests are served by maintaining the status quo?
3. Whose interests are served by change?

H. WHAT QUESTIONS STILL NEED TO BE ANSWERED?

Go through your list of "big questions."

1. Is there anything important that you feel is missing?
2. Does something strike you as peculiar?

3. Is there anything that you don't understand?

I. HAVE YOU FOUND ANY INTERESTING CONTROVERSIES?

1. Have you identified the issues on both sides of the controversy?
2. Who are the major participants? What is it about? Who are the writers defending each side?
3. How long ago did the controversy take place? Is it ongoing? Or is it of historical interest only?

J. WHO ARE YOU? WHAT ARE YOUR SPECIAL INTERESTS, EXPERIENCES, OR ABILITIES THAT COULD HELP YOU WRITE AN INTERESTING ESSAY?

1. Draw on your unique abilities to create an interesting and worthwhile paper.

EXAMPLE:

Imagine that you are taking a history class called "Renaissance and Reformation" because you need to fulfill your European history requirement. What can you find to write about?

a. If you are interested in science and technology, imagine writing a paper that shows how the invention of movable type affected the spread of Protestant ideas during the Reformation.

b. If you are interested in the theater, imagine writing a paper describing what happened to church festivals and passion plays after the Reformation.

c. If you are interested in business and finance, imagine writing a paper that shows how the financial demands of the Catholic church encouraged the spread of Protestantism in Europe.

K. HAVE YOU FOUND A TOPIC THAT DOES NOT SEEM TO BE FULLY EXPLORED IN THE GENERAL LITERATURE ON THE SUBJECT?

1. Have you found an authority, a teacher, or other professional who can help you write a paper on this topic?
2. Have you found sources such as books, articles, lab reports, etc. that contain information on your topic? You may not find a work that directly addresses your topic, but a work on a similar subject may contain useful information.

A book on the Peasant's Revolt of 1524–25 is likely to contain information about the conditions of the poor in the sixteenth century.

VII. Checklist

A. UNDERSTAND THE "BIG PICTURE."

Make sure that you have a fair amount of general knowledge about your subject area.

B. IDENTIFY THE "AUTHORITIES" IN THE FIELD.

C. WRITE DOWN A FAIRLY LONG LIST OF QUESTIONS THAT YOU WANT TO ASK ABOUT YOUR SUBJECT.

D. FORM SOME OPINIONS ABOUT YOUR SUBJECT.

E. IDENTIFY A NUMBER OF BROAD TOPICS WITHIN YOUR SUBJECT AREA.

F. TRY TO NARROW SOME OF THESE BROAD TOPICS INTO MORE MANAGEABLE SUBTOPICS.

G. IDENTIFY SOME TOPICS OF SPECIAL INTEREST TO YOU.

Chapter 2

How to Identify
a Topic Question

Finding a good topic question is the most important task in writing an essay. It is also the most neglected. Too often, students simply begin to write about their topics without realizing that they need to ask and answer a topic question and justify their point of view. The result is a disorganized and seemingly pointless essay that is difficult to write and boring to read.

A topic question, on the other hand, allows you to direct your research toward a realizable goal, to formulate a clear and coherent thesis statement, and to present your argument in an organized and logical manner.

Of course, finding a topic question is not easy; often, it is one of the hardest things that you will do. The best place to start is with the questions that you asked about your topic (see Chapter 1): How do you feel about the books you have read? Do you agree or disagree with the opinions of the leading authorities on your subject? Why is this topic particularly important and/or relevant at this time? Consider these questions, and see if you can add more to your list. Finally, ask yourself whether you can organize and write an answer to any of these questions. Why is it important and interesting to do so?

Tip: Ask *open-ended questions,* that is, questions that permit more than one possible answer. At this stage of the writing process, you do not need to formulate an answer to your topic question. You only need to ask it. Once you have done more research, you state your opinion in a formal *thesis statement*. Until then, however, it is important that you approach your topic with an open mind. You must be able to assess your evidence in an unbiased manner; you also must persuade your reader that you considered both sides of a controversial issue before you made up your mind.

I. What Is a Topic Question?

A topic question asks an important and relevant question about your topic that you answer in the form of a written essay.

A. YOUR TOPIC QUESTION MAY BE ONE THAT OTHER WRITERS OR SCIENTISTS HAVE CONSIDERED.

In this case, you will want to try to answer the question in a different way, perhaps by examining new sources of evidence.

EXAMPLE:

TOPIC:

The Economic Relationship between the United States and Brazil

POSSIBLE TOPIC QUESTIONS:

How important is Brazil as a destination for U.S. investment in South America?

Is there a case for extending American-style labor standards and environmental protection in Brazil?

How has the North American Free Trade Agreement (NAFTA) changed the United States' relationship with Brazil, our largest trading partner in Latin America?

B. YOUR TOPIC QUESTION MAY BE ONE YOU HAVE FORMULATED YOURSELF.

If so, you must explain (in the body of your essay) why it is an important question to ask at this time.

EXAMPLE:

TOPIC:

Bicycles and Their Impact on American Culture

POSSIBLE TOPIC QUESTIONS:

How did mass-produced bicycles change the lives of the working men and women in late nineteenth- and early twentieth-century America?

How have roads and highways changed to accommodate bicycle riders since their invention in the early nineteenth century?

How do we explain the popularity of the mountain bike in the 1970s and 1980s?

II. Why Is a Topic Question Important?

A. A TOPIC QUESTION ALLOWS YOU TO FOCUS YOUR TOPIC ON AN ISSUE OF PARTICULAR RELEVANCE TO YOU AND PRESUMABLY TO YOUR READERS.

B. A TOPIC QUESTION LEADS DIRECTLY TO YOUR THESIS STATEMENT.

When you answer your topic question, you state your judgment or opinion. This is your thesis statement.

EXAMPLE 1:

POSSIBLE TOPIC:

The Economic Relationship between the United States and Brazil

TOPIC QUESTION:

How has the North American Free Trade Agreement (NAFTA) changed the United States' relationship with Brazil, our largest trading partner in Latin America?

THESIS STATEMENT:

I believe that NAFTA has changed the United States' economic relationship with Brazil by encouraging the development of alternate regional trade alliances such as *Mercosur.*

EXAMPLE 2:

POSSIBLE TOPIC:

Bicycles and Their Impact on American Culture

TOPIC QUESTION:

How did mass-produced bicycles change the lives of the working men and women in late nineteenth- and early twentieth-century America?

THESIS STATEMENT:

Mass-produced bicycles changed the lives of working men and women by allowing them to travel beyond the confines of crowded urban areas like Boston and Philadelphia and to experience the countryside in an entirely new way.

C. A TOPIC QUESTION HELPS YOU TO IDENTIFY THE METHOD OF ANALYSIS THAT YOU WILL USE.

The various methods of analysis include *definition, description, process analysis, comparison, causation,* and *narration.* How you phrase your question directs the method of analysis you use. We will discuss methods of analysis in greater detail in Chapter 6.

D. A TOPIC QUESTION DIRECTS YOUR RESEARCH.

Without a topic question, you face the task of collecting and organizing seemingly random facts. A topic question, however, encourages you to collect only relevant pieces of information.

III. What Is a "Good" Topic Question?

A. A GOOD TOPIC QUESTION ASKS AN *IMPORTANT* QUESTION ABOUT A TOPIC.

Ask yourself, would *you* want to read an essay on this question? If you do not want to read it, you will not want to write it.

B. A GOOD TOPIC QUESTION IS AN OPEN-ENDED QUESTION THAT PERMITS MORE THAN ONE POSSIBLE ANSWER.

Formulate a question that could be answered in a number of different ways. This allows you to consider all sides of a controversial issue before making up your mind. It also shows your reader that you plan to assess your evidence in a fair and unbiased manner.

C. A GOOD TOPIC QUESTION CAN BE ANSWERED IN THE TIME AND SPACE AVAILABLE.

Ask yourself, "Do I have enough time to research this question? Do I have enough time to write a sufficiently lengthy essay on this topic?" If the answer is no to either question, you need either to change your question or to narrow the focus of your topic.

IV. How Do You Identify a "Good" Topic Question?

A. DO SOME BRAIN-STORMING AND WRITE DOWN AS MANY QUESTIONS AS POSSIBLE.

1. Ask "big picture questions" about your topic: Who? What? When? Where? Why? How? How much?

2. Do not censor yourself. At this point, you need only to identify possible topic questions; you do not need to answer them.

B. ASK THE ADVICE OF YOUR INSTRUCTOR OR A KNOWLEDGE-ABLE PROFESSIONAL.

Authorities in a given field or discipline are likely to know any number of interesting questions that you could ask about your topic.

V. How Do You Ask a Topic Question? Think about the Kind of Essay That You Want to Write ...

A. DO YOU WANT TO IDENTIFY A THEORY OR A SET OF BASIC PRINCIPLES AND USE IT TO SOLVE A PROBLEM?

In this case, your topic question should take the following form:

1. "How does the thesis presented by [a specific authority] help to explain the events I have observed?"

2. Or, "How do [a set of basic principles] help to explain the problem I have observed?"

EXAMPLE:

SUBJECT: Shakespeare's *Hamlet*

TOPIC: The Title Character in Shakespeare's *Hamlet*

TOPIC QUESTION:

How does Sigmund Freud's theory of human sexuality explain the internal conflict experienced by the title character in Shakespeare's *Hamlet*?

3. If you adopt this method of analysis, consider the following questions:

   a. Who uses this solution? Is it one person or a group of people?

   b. Is this the best possible way to solve the problem? Why?

   c. When was this method developed?

      (1) Has anything changed to make this solution less reliable than before?

      (2) Is this solution dated?

      Note: The preceding example, a Freudian analysis of Shakespeare's *Hamlet,* is *very* dated. It was first used by Ernest Jones in his *Hamlet and Oedipus* (1949).

   d. Why is it important to apply an existing solution to this problem? Why not develop a new solution?

B. DO YOU WANT TO DEVELOP A *NEW SOLUTION* THAT EXPLAINS A GIVEN SET OF FACTS?

In this case, your topic question should take the following form: "What [generalization] explains [a given set of facts]?"

EXAMPLE:

SUBJECT: Exploration of the North American Continent

   TOPIC: Lewis & Clark Expedition

      TOPIC QUESTION:

      How do we explain the collection of botanical specimens, animal skins, rock samples, and Native American artifacts by Meriwether Lewis and William Clark during their famous expedition along the Columbia and Missouri rivers?

C. DO YOU WANT TO FOCUS ON THE *DEFINITION* OF A WORD, TERM, OR CONCEPT?

In this case, your topic question should take the following form: "How do I define [a given word or idea]?"

EXAMPLE:

SUBJECT: Personal Qualities

   TOPIC: Courage

How do I define "courage"?

D. DO YOU WANT TO FOCUS ON THE *DESCRIPTION* OF A PERSON, PLACE, THING, OR SITUATION IN ORDER TO LEAVE THE READER WITH A DOMINANT IMPRESSION?

1. You can use a *simile, metaphor, analogy,* or *proverb.*
2. You also can use *sense impressions,* such as sight, sound, touch, taste, and smell.
3. Or you can use *internal physical and / or emotional experiences.*
4. Your topic question may take the following form: "How do I describe [a given word, idea, setting, person, etc.]?"

EXAMPLE:

SUBJECT: My Summer Vacation

TOPIC: A Day Spent at the Beach

TOPIC QUESTION:

How do I describe a summer day at the beach?

E. DO YOU WANT TO *DESCRIBE A REPEATABLE PROCESS* IN A STEP-BY-STEP FASHION?

This is often called *process analysis* and is the basis of all "how-to-do-it" books. In this case, your topic question should take the following form: "How do you [undertake a repeatable process]?"

EXAMPLE:

SUBJECT: Interviews

TOPIC: Job Interviews

TOPIC QUESTION:

How should a college student conduct an effective job interview?

F. DO YOU WANT TO FOCUS ON THE *COMPARISON* OR *CONTRAST* OF SOME ASPECT OF A PERSON, PLACE, THING, OR IDEA WITH THAT OF ANOTHER SIMILAR PERSON, PLACE, THING, OR IDEA IN ORDER TO DEMONSTRATE THEIR RELATIONSHIP?

In this case, your topic question should take the following form: "How is [one person, place, thing, or idea] [similar to or different from] another?"

SUBJECT: Students at Élite American Universities

> TOPIC: Freshmen Students at Élite American Universities
>
> > TOPIC QUESTION:
> >
> > How do freshmen students at the University of Chicago compare to freshmen students at Columbia University?

G. DO YOU WANT TO IDENTIFY THE *CAUSE(S)* OF A SPECIFIC EVENT?

In this case, your topic question should take the following forms:

1. "What factors combined to cause [a given event]?"
2. Or, "What was the most important factor to cause [a given event]?"

SUBJECT: The War on Poverty

> TOPIC: Private Industry and the War on Poverty
>
> > TOPIC QUESTION:
> >
> > What caused private industry to become heavily involved in the Job Corps, the residential vocation education and training component of the Economic Opportunity Act (1964)?

H. DO YOU WANT TO IDENTIFY THE *EFFECT(S)* OF A SPECIFIC EVENT?

In this case, your topic question should take the following forms:

1. "What were the effects of [a given event]?"
2. Or, "What was the most important effect of [a given event]?"
3. Or, "How did [a given event] affect [a person, place, thing, or event]?"

SUBJECT: The Landscape of the American West

Topic: Piñon-Juniper Woodlands in the American West

    Topic question:

    How has the spread of the Piñon pine affected the ecology and the social landscape of the American West?

I. DO YOU WANT TO *TELL THE STORY* OF HOW AN EVENT TOOK PLACE OR SITUATION CAME ABOUT?

In this case, your topic question should take the following form: "How did [a given event] develop or take place?"

EXAMPLE:

Subject: Jazz Music

    Topic: Swing-Style Music

        Topic question:

        How did "swing," a hot jazz-oriented style of dance music, come into existence?

VI. Evaluate Your Topic Question

A. IS YOUR TOPIC QUESTION TOO NARROW IN SCOPE?

1. If you cannot find much information on your topic question in your local college, university, or municipal library, your focus on the topic is probably too narrow.

2. You can broaden the focus of the topic question by relating it to a larger concept or a broader set of issues.

EXAMPLE:

Too specific a topic question:

What effect did China's involvement in the Korean War (1950–53) have on the implementation of Mao Tse-tung's Five-Year Plan?

Topic question broadened:

What political and economic circumstances affected the implementation of Mao Tse-tung's Five-Year Plan?

B. IS YOUR TOPIC QUESTION TOO BROAD IN SCOPE?

1. If you feel that you cannot do justice to your topic in the amount of time and space available, your focus on the topic is probably too broad.

2. You can narrow the focus of the topic question by relating it to a specific set of facts or examples.

EXAMPLE:

TOO BROAD A TOPIC QUESTION:

What are the effects of the North American Free Trade Agreement (NAFTA) on American workers?

TOPIC QUESTION NARROWED:

What are the effects of NAFTA on tomato growers in Florida and California?

C. **DO YOU HAVE THE RESOURCES NECESSARY TO ANSWER YOUR TOPIC QUESTION?**

1. Do you have access to the necessary library resources, archives, and/or lab materials?
2. Can a faculty member or other professional give you advice regarding your topic question? If not, consider changing your question.

VII. Checklist

A. **IDENTIFY ONE TOPIC OF SPECIAL INTEREST TO YOU.**

B. **THINK ABOUT THE VARIOUS *METHODS OF ANALYSIS* THAT YOU COULD USE TO ASK YOUR TOPIC QUESTION.**

The various methods of analysis include *definition, description, process analysis, comparison, causation,* and *narration.*

C. **ASK A TOPIC QUESTION.**

D. **EVALUATE YOUR TOPIC QUESTION.**

1. Why is this an important question to ask?
2. Do you have the resources available to answer this question in the time and space available?
3. Is your question too narrow in scope? Is it too broad in scope?
4. Have you stated your question fairly to allow room for disagreement?

Chapter 3

How to Write a Thesis Statement

Before you can formulate a thesis statement, you must start with a *topic question*. You cannot skip this essential step. If your instructor has assigned you an "essay question" (we call it a topic question), then you are ready to write a thesis statement. If you are writing a research paper, we suggest that you review Chapter 2, "How to Identify a Topic Question."

Next, you must find the courage to form an opinion and to state it, clearly and unequivocally. You might be wrong. But no one will fault you if you back up your opinion with authoritative evidence and logical reasoning.

Finally, you must (a) be sure that you have approached your evidence in an unbiased manner and (b) be sure that you consider both sides of a controversial question before making up your mind. These steps are very important. The point of writing an essay is to convince readers that your opinion or judgment on an issue is sound. You cannot do that if your readers distrust your handling of evidence or if they think that you have ignored opposing points of view.

Once you have established your topic question, courage, and objectivity, you are ready to write a *thesis statement*.

I. What Is a Thesis Statement?

A. A *THESIS STATEMENT* IS THE ANSWER TO YOUR TOPIC QUESTION.

The thesis statement presents your judgment or opinion about an issue. You cannot write an essay without one.

25

Tip: When you formulate your thesis statement, use the words, "I believe ..." or "In my opinion ...." This ensures that you are making a personal judgment. You can eliminate these phrases later when you are almost finished writing your essay.

EXAMPLE:

SUBJECT: Alexis de Tocqueville's *Democracy in America* (1835)

TOPIC QUESTION:

Why did Tocqueville think that American democracy was unique?

THESIS STATEMENT 1:

In my opinion, Tocqueville thought that American democracy was unique because it had been born without violent revolution, unlike democracy in France.

THESIS STATEMENT 2:

American democracy was unique, according to Tocqueville, because it had developed in response to historical and geographical circumstances that could not be found in any other nation.

THESIS STATEMENT 3:

I believe that Tocqueville considered American democracy to be unique because it had a government that combined the strength and progressiveness of a large country with the prosperity and freedom of a small one.

II. What Is a "Good" Thesis Statement?

A. A GOOD THESIS STATEMENT IS SHORT AND SIMPLE.

It should be no more than one sentence long, regardless of the length of your essay.

EXAMPLE:

TOPIC QUESTION:

According to Tocqueville, what is the role of "the people" in a modern democracy?

WRONG: THESIS STATEMENT THAT IS TOO LONG.

Tocqueville believed that "the people" take an indirect role in government. Except in small communities like townships in New England, they do not actively participate in government. Instead, they fulfill their obligations as citizens by electing representatives and by allowing those individuals to make laws.

CORRECT: THESIS STATEMENT.

Tocqueville believed that "the people" take an indirect role in a modern democracy by choosing representatives rather than by actively participating in government.

B. A GOOD THESIS STATEMENT IS LIMITED TO ONE MAIN IDEA ABOUT YOUR TOPIC.

Unless your topic question is far too narrow, one main idea should give you enough material to fill up the required number of pages.

EXAMPLE:

TOPIC QUESTION:

How does American democracy promote both political equality and equality of conditions?

WRONG: THESIS STATEMENT WITH MORE THAN ONE MAIN IDEA.

I believe that American democracy promotes both political equality and equality of conditions through the mechanism of a strong central government, and I also believe that this emphasis on equality is an important reason why democratic society in America is similar to democratic society in postrevolutionary France.

CORRECT: THESIS STATEMENT.

I believe that American democracy promotes both political equality and equality of conditions through the mechanism of a strong central government.

C. A GOOD THESIS STATEMENT IS A DECLARATIVE SENTENCE THAT CONTAINS *NO* QUALIFIERS.

Qualifiers are words like "maybe," "seems like," "possibly." They indicate that you are afraid to make a judgment. Have courage! Take a stand! We will show you how to support your position in Part II of this book.

EXAMPLE:

TOPIC QUESTION:

Why did Tocqueville consider aristocracy to be superior to democracy?

WRONG: THESIS STATEMENT WITH QUALIFIERS.

Tocqueville might have thought that aristocracy was superior to democracy because it provides leadership by an educated élite.

CORRECT: THESIS STATEMENT.

Tocqueville thought that aristocracy was superior to democracy because it provides leadership by an educated élite, thereby contributing to political stability.

III. How Do You Write a Good Thesis Statement?

A. WRITE SEVERAL TRIAL THESIS STATEMENTS.

You do not write a "perfect" thesis statement on your first try. Instead, you have to write and rewrite both your topic question and your thesis statement a number of times in different ways. It is important to remember that your thesis statement is not written in stone. At this stage, it is only a "working hypothesis," which allows you to gather your evidence and to organize your argument. If it does not work, change it.

B. IF YOU ARE UNSURE OF WHAT POSITION TO TAKE ON A CONTROVERSIAL ISSUE, TRY WRITING YOUR THESIS STATEMENT FROM TWO DIFFERENT POINTS OF VIEW. THEN, DECIDE WHICH ONE BEST REPRESENTS YOUR OPINION.

If you still cannot decide, try listing the facts that support each case. Then decide which argument seems more persuasive.

EXAMPLE:

TOPIC QUESTION:

Did Tocqueville believe that other countries could adopt American-style democratic principles and institutions?

TRIAL THESIS STATEMENT ON ONE SIDE OF AN ISSUE:

Tocqueville believed that countries could adopt other American-style democratic principles and institutions.

TRIAL THESIS STATEMENT ON THE OTHER SIDE OF AN ISSUE:

Tocqueville believed that American democracy was unique and that other countries could not successfully adopt it.

IV. Evaluate Your Thesis Statement

A. HAVE YOU MERELY RESTATED THE TOPIC QUESTION WITHOUT ANSWERING IT?

EXAMPLE:

Topic question:

Did Tocqueville consider aristocracy to be the best form of government? If so, why? If not, why not?

Wrong: Restatement of the topic question.

In this essay, we examine whether or not Tocqueville thought aristocracy to be the best form of government.

Correct: Thesis statement.

Tocqueville thought that aristocracy was the best form of government because it provided leadership by an educated élite, it produced effective administrative centralization, and it promoted superior intellectual and artistic achievements.

B. HAVE YOU TRIED TO ARGUE BOTH SIDES OF A CASE?

EXAMPLE:

Topic question:

Did Tocqueville consider aristocracy to be the best form of government? If so, why? If not, why not?

Wrong: Arguing for both sides of the case.

Although Tocqueville saw some advantages to aristocratic government, he also saw some disadvantages.

Correct: Thesis statement.

Tocqueville saw both the advantages and disadvantages of aristocratic government, but he still maintained that it was the best form of government for France.

C. HAVE YOU PREJUDGED THE ISSUE BY USING *LOADED LANGUAGE?*

Writers use *loaded language* when they want to manipulate their readers' emotions in order to keep them from paying close attention to the logical flaws in their argument. Most of the time, they do not fool anyone.

EXAMPLE:

Topic question:

How did Tocqueville's social background affect his attitude toward democratic institutions?

WRONG: PREJUDGING THE ISSUE BY USING LOADED LANGUAGE.

Tocqueville was born with a silver spoon in his mouth; so he could not understand that democracy is the best form of government.

CORRECT: THESIS STATED FAIRLY.

Tocqueville's background as a French aristocrat made him particularly critical of democratic institutions.

D. HAVE YOU WRITTEN A BLAND, BORING THESIS STATEMENT?

Remember, a thesis statement is always emphatic! It is never wishy-washy! Use an exclamation point to check your sentence.

EXAMPLE:

TOPIC QUESTION:

To what extent did Tocqueville undermine his own arguments in favor of aristocratic government?

WRONG: THESIS STATEMENT THAT LACKS EMPHASIS.

In some ways, Tocqueville undermined his own arguments in favor of aristocratic government by showing that democratic government generally produces good citizens.

CORRECT: THESIS STATEMENT.

Tocqueville undermined his own arguments in favor of aristocratic government by showing that democratic government produces patriotic citizens committed to the preservation of liberty and equality!

V. Checklist

A. START WITH A TOPIC QUESTION.

B. ANSWER YOUR TOPIC QUESTION IN A NUMBER OF DIFFERENT WAYS (TRIAL THESIS STATEMENTS).

C. CHOOSE THE TRIAL THESIS STATEMENT THAT BEST SUITS YOUR EVIDENCE.

D. EVALUATE YOUR THESIS STATEMENT.

   1. Is it a short and simple sentence?
   2. Is it limited to one main idea about your topic?

Part II

PROVE YOUR ARGUMENT

An academic essay is assigned to enable a student to learn three things:

1. How to explore a subject area and to make a judgment about a particular issue.
2. **How to create an argument supporting that judgment using reasoning and evidence.**
3. How to write an interesting and coherently organized essay.

The first, and possibly the most important, stage in the production of an essay is the formation of a clear and coherent topic question and thesis statement. This is the focus of the first part of our book. The next stage is the creation of a logical *argument* that is supported by both reasoning and evidence. This is what we will focus on next.

The argument and the written essay are *not* the same thing. The *argument* is a laundry list of all the elements you need to consider *before* you even think about writing the essay. It allows you to organize the pieces of the research puzzle, separating the bits that are irrelevant and fitting together the others to form a coherent whole.

This section shows you the steps in making a logical argument. Chapter 4, "How to Use Evidence," provides tips on how to use facts, quotes, anecdotes, statistics, and other types of evidence to make your argument ring true. Chapter 5, "How to Use Reasoning," explores some of the basic principles of reasoning. Finally, Chapter 6, "How to Structure an Argument," shows you how to use reasoning to develop a coherent argument.

How to Use Evidence

At this point, you should have a topic question and a thesis statement. The next thing you need is *evidence* to convince your reader that your judgment is sound.

You should be gathering information, or evidence, from the moment you begin exploring your topic. Without it, you can neither write a topic question nor develop a thesis statement. Why do you include it in your essay? You include it to show your reader at least some of the information that you used to form an opinion about your topic. When readers are allowed to view your research and to follow your logical chain of reasoning, they are far less likely to challenge your essay.

Evidence comes in a variety of shapes and sizes, from direct quotes to authoritative facts, from illustrations to graphs and statistics. As you might already know, all facts are not equal. Some readers are more convinced by "scientific" evidence such as statistics than by anecdotal evidence, despite the fact that stories often illustrate key points in ways that numbers cannot. You have to choose the most effective type of evidence.

Do not manipulate your evidence to make it support your thesis. If the evidence does not support your thesis, then you must change your thesis to accommodate your evidence!

I. What Is Evidence?

A. EVIDENCE CONSISTS OF FACTS, OPINIONS, ANECDOTES, ILLUSTRATIONS, AND/OR CLARIFYING EXAMPLES THAT SUPPORT YOUR THESIS STATEMENT.

Each item of "evidence" must lend support to your thesis statement. It also must be related in some way to your topic question.

1. *Facts* are most frequently used as evidence in academic essays. They may include names, dates, events and other specific pieces of information.

TOPIC QUESTION:

How have new discoveries in physics changed our perception of the natural world?

THESIS STATEMENT:

New discoveries in physics have caused us to view the material world as a shifting array of objects that we cannot hold in our gaze.

SUPPORTING EVIDENCE:

FACT:

J. J. Thompson's discovery of the electron in 1897 showed that the atom was not indivisible, as its Greek name had implied, but could be broken down into its constituent parts.

TOPIC QUESTION:

How did eighteenth-century Englishmen and -women feel about their children?

THESIS STATEMENT:

Eighteenth-century parents doted on their children, expressing their feelings in a highly sentimental manner.

SUPPORTING EVIDENCE:

FACT:

James Nelson, in his popular *Essay on the Government of Children,* published in the 1750s, wrote that parents were more likely to be excessively permissive than overly strict.

2. *Authoritative opinions* can also be used as evidence to support your argument. These may include the opinions of authorities in the field or your own opinions as long as they are solidly grounded in fact.

THESIS STATEMENT:

New discoveries in physics have caused us to view the material world as a shifting array of objects that we cannot hold in our gaze.

SUPPORTING EVIDENCE:

OPINION:

Modern artists—in particular, futurist and cubist painters—used new discoveries in physics to portray the material world as matter in motion.

EXAMPLE 2:

THESIS STATEMENT:

Eighteenth-century parents doted on their children, expressing their feelings in a highly sentimental manner.

SUPPORTING EVIDENCE:

OPINION:

In Reynolds' portrait of *Mrs. Hester Thrale and Her Daughter Queeney* (1781), mother and daughter do not adopt stiff and formal poses; instead, they appear affectionate, even devoted.

3. *Quotable comments* are also useful as evidence. However, do not rely heavily on quotes to establish a point since they can be misleading. A quote represents only one point of view, and it may or may not be representative of a larger body of opinion. Be sure that your quote comes from an authoritative source.

EXAMPLE 1:

THESIS STATEMENT:

New discoveries in physics have caused us to view the material world as a shifting array of objects that we cannot hold in our gaze.

SUPPORTING EVIDENCE:

QUOTE:

J. Bronowski, the popular historian of science, wrote that "we devise more precise instruments with which to observe nature with more fineness. And when we look at the observations, we are discomfited to see that they are still fuzzy, and we feel that they are as uncertain as ever. We seem to be running after a goal which lurches away from us to infinity every time we come within sight of it." (*The Ascent of Man,* 1973).

EXAMPLE 2:

THESIS STATEMENT:

Eighteenth-century parents doted on their children, expressing their feelings in a highly sentimental manner.

SUPPORTING EVIDENCE:

QUOTE:

Lady Kildare said of her children, "are not my pretty babes a blessing? When I look round at them all, does not my heart rejoice at the sight, and overflow with tenderness?"

4. *Anecdotes,* or short stories, can enliven an academic essay; they can also make an argument ring true.

EXAMPLE 1:

THESIS STATEMENT:

New discoveries in physics have caused us to view the material world as a shifting array of objects that we cannot hold in our gaze.

SUPPORTING EVIDENCE:

ANECDOTE:

In the 1920s, university professors struggling to understand the new physics developed the Principle of Uncertainty: on Mondays, Wednesdays, and Fridays the electron would behave as a particle; on Tuesdays, Thursdays, and Saturdays it would behave like a wave.

EXAMPLE 2:

THESIS STATEMENT:

Eighteenth-century parents doted on their children, expressing their feelings in a highly sentimental manner.

SUPPORTING EVIDENCE:

ANECDOTE:

Henry Fox, Secretary of War under King George II, was also a devoted father who spoiled and indulged his children. When his eldest son insisted on taking apart a watch fob, Fox merely murmured, "Well, if you must, you must."

II. What Kind of Evidence Will You Need?

A. YOU WILL NEED EVIDENCE THAT SUPPORTS YOUR THESIS STATEMENT.

B. YOU WILL NEED EVIDENCE THAT SUPPORTS THE *RELEVANT ISSUES* THAT YOU WILL DISCUSS IN THE BODY OF YOUR PAPER.

Relevant issues are questions that are directly related to your topic question. They allow you to extend the scope of your analysis without straying from the main point.

EXAMPLE:

TOPIC QUESTION:

What was Tocqueville's attitude toward democracy?

MAIN ISSUE:

Tocqueville's Attitude toward Democracy

RELEVANT ISSUES:

a. What were contemporary attitudes toward democracy?

   (1) Besides Tocqueville, what were the attitudes of other nine-teenth-century authors toward democracy?

   (a) Did Tocqueville read any works of other authors?

   (b) Was he acquainted with the authors of these works?

b. What political events might have shaped Tocqueville's attitudes toward democracy?

   (1) What was the political situation in Tocqueville's native country of France?

   (2) When and where did Tocqueville see "democracy" in action?

c. What are some personal factors that might have shaped Tocqueville's attitude toward democracy?

   (1) What was Tocqueville's position in society?

d. What attitude(s) did Tocqueville express about democracy in his writings?

   (1) Did he imply anything that he did not state directly?

e. How do various authorities on the subject, such as historians or political scientists, view Tocqueville's attitude toward democracy?

   (1) Do you agree with their interpretations?

III. How Do You Organize Your Evidence?

A. EVIDENCE IS ORGANIZED INTO DISTINCT UNITS CALLED PARAGRAPHS.

A paragraph contains one important idea that supports your argument. That idea, in turn, is supported by specific facts.

1. The *topic sentence* is a general statement, or argument, that you intend to prove in the body of the paragraph. It is always the first sentence of the paragraph.

2. Your *evidence* is contained in the body of the paragraph. It must support both your topic sentence and your overall argument.

3. When organizing your evidence within the paragraph, start with the most *general* statements and conclude with the most specific facts.

EXAMPLE 1:

TOPIC QUESTION:

How did contact with the New World shape European consciousness in the late fifteenth and sixteenth centuries?

THESIS STATEMENT:

Contact with Africa and the New World caused Europeans to critique the values of their own society.

TOPIC SENTENCE:

Michel de Montaigne (1533–92), a French essayist, used observations of Native American peoples to show the inequalities of wealth in European society.

EVIDENCE (GENERAL):

In his essay, "On Cannibals," Montaigne compared the equality of wealth enjoyed by Native Americans with the inequalities experienced by Europeans.

EVIDENCE (SPECIFIC):

He wrote that Native Americans appeared shocked by the fact that "there were among us men full and gorged with all sorts of good things to their heart's content, while their halves, haggard with hunger and poverty, stood begging at the doors."

COMPLETE PARAGRAPH:

Michel de Montaigne (1533–92), a French essayist, used observations of Native American peoples to show the inequalities of wealth in European society. In his essay, "On Cannibals," he compared the equality of wealth enjoyed by the natives with the inequalities experienced by Europeans. He wrote that the former appeared shocked by the fact that "there were among us men full and gorged with all sorts of good things to their heart's content, while their halves, haggard with hunger and poverty, stood begging at the doors."

EXAMPLE 2:

TOPIC QUESTION:

How does the transportation structure of Los Angeles (i.e., roads and freeways) affect the residents of that city?

THESIS STATEMENT:

In my opinion, the transportation structure of Los Angeles gives residents of that city both spatial freedom and economic opportunity.

TOPIC SENTENCE:

Los Angeles freeways are designed to allow residents to commute across the greater metropolitan area with relative ease.

EVIDENCE (GENERAL):

An hour's drive from any point in the region makes hundreds of possible employers accessible.

EVIDENCE (SPECIFIC):

Workers can live in the San Fernando Valley and work in the old industrial sector in Los Angeles, or they can commute from suburban Glendale to the beach city of Santa Monica.

TRANSITION:

This allows residents greater job opportunities than are found in other major cities.

COMPLETE PARAGRAPH:

Los Angeles freeways are designed to allow residents to commute across the greater metropolitan area with relative ease. An hour's drive from any point in the region makes hundreds of possible employers accessible. Workers can live in the San Fernando Valley and work in the old industrial sector in Los Angeles, or they can commute from Pasadena to the beach city of Santa Monica. This allows residents greater job opportunities than are found in other major cities.

IV. What Are the Rules of Evidence?

A. EACH FACT MUST BE ACCURATE.

1. Be sure that you have not made an error when copying down a quote or a piece of information, particularly dates and the spelling of names.

2. Treat statistics with caution. As one wit noted, "There are lies, damned lies, and statistics."

3. Do not use quotes out of context. A quote taken from a primary source, an article, or a book must reflect the meaning that its author intended it to have. You must not manipulate evidence for your own purposes!

B. EACH FACT MUST BE AUTHORITATIVE.

In other words, you must be sure that your source of information is reliable.

1. Each piece of information you use must come from a reliable source, such as from an author who is known for reporting the facts accurately and without bias. Reliable sources are often recognized as authorities in their fields.

2. If you use information that is related by an author who is biased, then you must acknowledge that fact. Using information from a biased source weakens your argument and leaves it open to challenge.

3. Avoid material that is obviously dated. Try to find the latest and most complete edition of a textbook or primary source. Be sure that your information has not been revised or updated by later research.

C. EACH FACT MUST BE RELEVANT.

Do not use facts or issues that are irrelevant to your argument.

EXAMPLE:

TOPIC QUESTION:

How did the devaluation of the Mexican *peso* in 1995 affect the trade relationship between the United States and Mexico?

RELEVANT ISSUE(S):

The devaluation of the Mexican peso in 1995

The trade relationship between the United States and Mexico

IRRELEVANT ISSUE(S):

The price fluctuations of the Japanese *yen*

The trade relationship between the United States and Canada

D. THE NUMBER OF FACTS MUST BE ADEQUATE TO PROVE YOUR POINT.

1. The quantity of evidence that you present depends on the nature of your argument. If your thesis is controversial, you need to present a good deal of evidence to make your argument convincing. If your thesis is uncontroversial (or if the point you are making is fairly obvious), you need to present only as much evidence as you think necessary to convince your reader.

2. Use sufficient evidence to support your point. If you do not have enough facts, you appear to be "leaping to a conclusion."

3. Beware of using too much evidence. You risk losing your readers in a mass of detail.

E. THE FACTS MUST BE ARRANGED IN A WAY THAT BEST PROVES YOUR POINT.

1. *Logical order* includes, but is not limited to:
   a. General to specific.
   b. Specific to general.
   c. Simple to complex.
   d. Complex to simple.
   e. Most important to least important.
   f. Least important to most important.

2. *Climactic order* includes, but is not limited to:
   a. Least exciting to most exciting.
   b. Most exciting to least exciting.

3. *Chronological order* includes earliest event to most recent event.

V. What If Your Evidence Is Weak?

A. **WHAT IF MY EVIDENCE DOES NOT SUPPORT A PARTICULAR POINT?**

   1. When the point is *crucial* to your argument, you can acknowledge the problem in one of two ways:

      a. You can argue that the evidence does not tell the whole truth.

      b. You can describe what you expected to find and what, in fact, you found. Then you can draw conclusions from your investigation.

   2. When the point is *relevant* to your argument, but not crucial, you have to evaluate its importance to your overall argument.

      a. You may eliminate the relevant point and use other points to support your argument.

      b. You may keep the relevant point and acknowledge your difficulties with the evidence.

        (1) When the problem is substantial, acknowledge your difficulties in the body of your paper.

        (2) When the problem is minor, explain your difficulties in a footnote.

B. **DO NOT MANIPULATE YOUR EVIDENCE TO MAKE IT SUPPORT YOUR THESIS.**

If you manipulate your evidence, you destroy both the validity of the work and your reputation. If the evidence does not support your thesis, then you should change your thesis to accommodate your evidence.

   1. Do not overlook significant factors, individuals, or events.

   2. Do not ignore evidence that appears to undermine your thesis.

   3. Do not make a generalization based on inadequate facts.

   4. Do not make a false generalization by arguing that:

      a. What is true of one part must be true of the whole.

      b. What is true of the whole must be true of one part.

5. Do not assume that the majority opinion is correct.

6. Do not make an inference or a conclusion that does not follow from established points or evidence. This is called a *non sequitur* ("it does not follow").

VI. Expect to Be Challenged

You must expect your teacher, reader, or listener to find exceptions to your points and to bring up every mistake you make in the use of reasoning and evidence. Be prepared to respond.

VII. Checklist

A. GATHER DIFFERENT TYPES OF EVIDENCE, FROM ANEC-DOTES AND ILLUSTRATIONS TO QUOTES AND STATISTICS.

B. SELECT EVIDENCE TO SUPPORT YOUR THESIS STATEMENT.

C. SELECT EVIDENCE TO SUPPORT THE RELEVANT ISSUES THAT YOU DISCUSS IN THE BODY OF YOUR PAPER.

D. ORGANIZE YOUR EVIDENCE INTO PARAGRAPHS.

E. MAKE SURE THAT YOU HAVE FOLLOWED THE RULES OF EVI-DENCE.

1. Is each fact accurate?

2. Is each fact authoritative?

3. Is each fact relevant?

4. Are the number of facts adequate to prove your point?

5. Are the facts arranged in a way that best proves your point?

F. DETERMINE WHETHER ANY OF YOUR EVIDENCE IS WEAK.

Chapter 5

How to Use Reasoning

How often have you heard these phrases? "Why don't you listen to reason?" "Don't you have any good sense?" All too often, this is our introduction to the concept of *reasoning*. These phrases imply that the ability to *reason*, or to think logically, is a gift that some people have and others do not. This is simply not true. The ability to reason is not a gift, but a learned skill. Every time you ask a question, accumulate facts or opinions, and make a decision based on those facts and opinions, you are reasoning.

The essay is a product of the kind of reasoning that you use every day. When you formulate your topic question and thesis statement, you are using logical processes known as *inquiry* and *inductive reasoning*. You use basic principles of *classification* to organize your argument. From time to time, you make use of *deductive reasoning*. Once you understand these basic principles, you find it much easier to write and to structure a clear and coherent essay.

I. What Is Reasoning?

A. SIMPLY PUT, REASONING IS THE WAY IN WHICH WE TRY TO ORGANIZE THE VARIOUS FACTS, OPINIONS, AND EXPERIENCES THAT WE DEAL WITH EVERY DAY.

II. What Are the Foundations of Reasoning?

A. INQUIRY.

Inquiry is the process by which we identify the facts, opinions, and experiences that we are particularly interested in exploring. It involves asking *questions* about our subject, questions that might be as simple as, "What is this?" or "Why did that happen?" Inquiry is particularly important in helping you to form a thesis statement and to make an argument.

1. Questions help to define the boundaries of a topic.

2. Questions limit the kinds of facts and/or opinions that you collect. For example, when you are researching your topic you collect only the facts that are related to your topic question.

3. Questions always precede any attempt to name concepts, to organize them into categories, or to make decisions.

4. Questions help you to identify the facts that are missing from your system of classification.

5. Questions help you to reorganize your thinking.

B. CLASSIFICATION.

To answer questions, we first refer to our own personal system of *classification,* which is composed of all the data we have accumulated over the years. When we use our system of classification to answer a question, we *compare* the characteristics of the information that interests us with the characteristics of objects or ideas that we already have a name for. Then we look to see if there is any correspondence.

1. If the information appears to be *similar* to objects or ideas that we have a name for, then we classify the information accordingly.

EXAMPLE:
It walked like a duck and quacked like a duck, therefore it must have been a duck.

2. If the information appears to be *different,* then we give it an arbitrary name and classify the information in a larger category.

EXAMPLE:
It looked like a duck, but it had very unusual markings and it did not have webbed feet. Therefore, I am going to call it "the bird that I saw on Bantam Lake last Thursday" and I am going to classify it as a variety of waterfowl.

C. CONCEPTS.

A classification system is made up of *concepts* that depend on language and culture for their meaning.

1. A single concept can have several different names, or *synonyms*.
2. Some concepts are easily translatable into other languages.

EXAMPLE:

Mother, electricity, car, love, country, head of state

3. Other concepts are not easily translatable.

EXAMPLE:

The Eskimo language has approximately thirty-seven words for a concept that, in English, is represented by a single word: snow.

D. ABSTRACTION.

The organization of a system of classification is based on the principle of *abstraction*.

1. When a concept accurately describes the object or information in question, it is said to be *concrete* or *specific*. When a concept only vaguely describes the object or information in question, it is said to be *abstract* or *general*.

EXAMPLE:

"West Highland Terrier," "dog," and "animal" are all *concepts,* each at a different level of abstraction. The list proceeds from the least abstract concept, "West Highland Terrier," to the most abstract concept, "animal."

2. The principle of abstraction allows concepts to be arranged in a system. They can be grouped according to their similarities, forming *classes* or larger *categories*.

   a. The concepts within a class must be similar in some basic way.

   b. Each class must be different from other classes within a larger category.

E. COMPARISON.

When concepts are at different levels of abstraction, order is established by *comparing* one concept with another.

1. When comparing two concepts, you need to identify the one that is more abstract.

The concept "animal" is more abstract than the concept "dog." The concept "dog" is more abstract than the concept "West Highland Terrier."

2. You can express the comparison in a number of ways.

You can say that "West Highland Terrier" is a more *concrete,* or *specific,* concept than the concept "dog."

You can say that the concept "dog" is more *general* than the concept "West Highland Terrier."

3. You can express this relationship in a standard outline form. Each letter or numeral in the outline represents a class or category that is at a different level of abstraction.

I. Animal
   A. Dog
      1. West Highland Terrier
         a. Katie Dog
         b. [Other names of individual West Highland Terriers]
      2. Scottish Terriers
         a. Mac
         b. [Other names of individual Scottish Terriers]
   B. Cat
      1. Persian
         a. Fred
         b. [Other names of individual Persian cats]

F. PRINCIPLES OF CLASSIFICATION.

When concepts are at the same level of abstraction, you must choose an ordering principle of classification that is appropriate to the kinds of data you are using. You could order concepts by number, color, relative importance, size, shape, etc.

The telephone book lists all subscribers alphabetically by name. The ordering is based on the generalization that people know the name of the subscriber that they wish to call.

G. PROPOSITIONS.

The establishment of order, or a system of classification, allows us to make an assertion, or a *proposition,* about the relationships between classes or categories of concepts. A proposition always takes the form of a declarative sentence.

EXAMPLE:

1. All [subject] is [predicate]. This is called the *universal affirmative.*
    a. All [war] is [devastating to the people of the country where it is fought].
    b. All [democracies] are [the best governments for mankind].
2. No [subject] is [predicate]. This is called the *universal negative.*
    a. No [war] is [an unmixed blessing for the winning side].
    b. No [democracies] are [effective without participation by the people].

III. What Are Some Reasoning Patterns?

When we "reason" we use many different patterns of thought. Two patterns that are of crucial importance in essay writing are *deductive* and *inductive reasoning.* These patterns help us to answer questions that we could not answer through direct observation.

A. DEDUCTIVE REASONING.

Deduction allows you to reason from a general to a specific concept within a system of classification.

EXAMPLE:

THE CASE:

A friend tells me that she has a new dog, a West Highland Terrier named Katie Dog. I wonder, "What color is Katie Dog?" There are two ways that I could answer this question. I could either go to my friend's house and observe the dog, or I could use the process of deductive reasoning to determine the color of the dog's coat.

THE ANALYSIS:

To use deductive reasoning, I ask a question about the more general category to which Katie Dog belongs. Instead of asking, "What color is Katie Dog?" I ask "What color is a West Highland Terrier?" After consulting a reference book that lists characteristics of specific breeds of dogs, I determine that all West Highland Terriers are white. I then make an *inference* (or conclusion) is that Katie Dog is white.

THE PATTERN OF ANALYSIS:

The conventional format for deductive reasoning is called the *syllogism:*

Generalization:	All West Highland Terriers are white.
Specific instance:	Katie Dog is a West Highland Terrier.
Conclusion (or inference):	Katie Dog is white.

B. INDUCTIVE REASONING.

Inductive reasoning is also known as "the scientific method" because it allows you to reason from a specific group of concepts to a more general one. It requires you to collect a number of facts, to identify their common characteristics, and to make a general statement (or *generalization*) based on those common characteristics.

EXAMPLE:

THE CASE:

Katie Dog wags her tail, makes a whining noise, jumps up and scratches my leg, and looks at me intently. My question is, "What does Katie Dog want?" Since I cannot ask her and expect to receive a reply, I must resort to inductive reasoning.

THE ANALYSIS:

First, I list the *facts* in my possession:

Katie Dog keeps jumping up and scratching my leg, she wags her tail, she makes a whining noise, and she looks intently at me.

Then, I identify the *common characteristics:*

Katie Dog behaves like this at noon every day.

I eliminate possible alternative explanations:

Katie Dog cannot be hungry since she has already eaten breakfast.

I still cannot be sure of what Katie Dog wants, but I can make an *inductive leap* from the facts that I know—across facts that I do not know—to reach a *conclusion,* or a generalization:

Katie Dog wants to go outside and play ball.

THE PATTERN OF ANALYSIS:

Specific facts:	Katie Dog wags her tail, makes a whining noise, jumps up and scratches my leg, and looks at me intently.
Common characteristics:	Katie Dog behaves like this at noon every day.
Conclusion (inference):	Katie Dog wants to go outside and play ball.

IV. Checklist.

In the next chapter, we will show you how to use these basic principles of reasoning to organize and structure your essay. In the meantime, consider what we do when we reason:

A. WE GIVE NAMES TO INDIVIDUAL PERSONS, PLACES, THINGS, FACTS, IDEAS, AND GROUPS OF RELATED INDIVIDUALS. THESE WE CALL *CONCEPTS.*

B. WE ARRANGE CONCEPTS INTO A *SYSTEM OF CLASSIFICA-TION* BASED ON THE *PRINCIPLE OF ABSTRACTION.*

C. WHEN WE WISH TO USE A NUMBER OF CONCEPTS AT THE SAME LEVEL OF ABSTRACTION, WE CHOOSE AN APPROPRI-ATE *ORDERING PRINCIPLE.*

D. WE ORGANIZE OUR THOUGHTS BY ASKING QUESTIONS, OR BY USING THE LOGICAL PROCESS CALLED *INQUIRY.*

E. WE USE *DEDUCTIVE REASONING* TO REASON FROM A *GEN-ERAL* TO A *SPECIFIC* CONCEPT WITHIN A SYSTEM OF CLAS-SIFICATION.

F. WE USE *INDUCTIVE REASONING* TO REASON FROM A *SPE-CIFIC* GROUP OF CONCEPTS TO A MORE *GENERAL* ONE.

Chapter 6

How to Structure an Argument

In this chapter, we show you how to structure your essay using inductive and deductive reasoning. If you have not read Chapter 5, "How to Use Reasoning," we suggest that you do so now.

First, you need to identify the *method of analysis* that you plan to use in your essay. To do this, consider the kind of topic question that you have chosen to ask. Did you seek to develop a new *solution* that explains a given set of facts? Did you focus on the *definition* of a word, term, or concept? Did you try to identify the *cause* or the *effect* of a specific event? Your choice determines the structure of your argument.

Next, you should read carefully through the following examples. In each case, we describe the reasoning process that you will use to develop a logical analysis. We also show you how to turn your analysis into a *written argument*. Never forget that the point of writing an essay is to convince your reader that your point of view is correct. The only way to do this is to organize a clear and logical argument.

I. What Is a *Method of Analysis*?

A method of analysis represents a particular approach to the essay. Various methods include *definition, description, process analysis, comparison, causation,* and *narration.* For information on how such methods are used to formulate topic questions, see Chapter 2.

II. How to Develop Your Analysis

To develop your analysis, ask yourself a series of questions.

A. DOES YOUR TOPIC QUESTION REQUIRE YOU TO APPLY *EXISTING KNOWLEDGE* TO A GIVEN BODY OF INFORMATION?

Often, a topic question requires you to identify a theory or set of basic principles and use it to solve a specific problem. In this case, you want to use *deductive reasoning* to organize your thinking.

EXAMPLE:

TOPIC QUESTION:

Does [a theory or set of basic principles] explain [a given event or situation]?

EXAMPLE:

Does [Sigmund Freud's theory of human sexuality] explain [the internal conflict experienced by William Shakespeare's character, Hamlet]?[1]

ANALYSIS USING DEDUCTIVE REASONING:

GENERALIZATION:

I show that [a theory or set of basic principles] explains certain events or situations.

EXAMPLE:

I show that [Freud's theory of human sexuality] explains [psychoneurosis: a state of mind where a person is deeply influenced by the "unconscious" part of the mind that has lain buried since early childhood].

SPECIFIC EXAMPLE:

I argue that [a given event or situation] is [one of these events or situations].

EXAMPLE:

I argue that [Hamlet's internal conflict] is [an example of psychoneurosis].

CONCLUSION:

I conclude that [a theory or set of basic principles] explains [a given event or situation].

---

[1]An elaboration of this argument can be found in Ernest Jones' *Hamlet and Oedipus* (1949).

I conclude that [Sigmund Freud's theory of human sexuality] explains [the internal conflict experienced by Hamlet].

FROM ANALYSIS TO ARGUMENT:

Note that the conclusion now becomes the thesis statement.

I. INTRODUCTION

    A. TOPIC QUESTION:

    Does Sigmund Freud's theory of human sexuality explain the internal conflict experienced by William Shakespeare's character, Hamlet?

    B. THESIS STATEMENT:

    I will argue that Sigmund Freud's theory of human sexuality explains the internal conflict experienced by Hamlet.

II. DISCUSSION

    A. GENERALIZATION:

    Freud's theory of human sexuality explains psychoneurosis: a state of mind where a person is deeply influenced by the "unconscious" part of the mind that has lain buried since early childhood.

    1. POINT 1:

    Freud suggests that early childhood experiences, particularly sexual ones, have an important effect on the unconscious mind.

        a. EVIDENCE:

        Freud suggests that the earliest sexual experience may be an attraction between mother and son.

    2. POINT 2:

    Freud suggests that the unconscious mind influences human behavior.

        a. EVIDENCE:

        Freud suggests that the attraction exercised by the mother may exert a controlling influence over the son's later life.

    B. SPECIFIC EXAMPLE:

    Hamlet's internal conflict is an example of psychoneurosis.

    1. POINT 1:

    Hamlet's early childhood experiences, particularly his relationship with his mother, have an important effect on his unconscious mind.

a. EVIDENCE:

Hamlet's love for Ophelia is an unconscious attempt to replicate his relationship with his mother.

2. POINT 2:

Hamlet's unconscious, or "repressed," sexual desire for his mother affects his behavior.

a. EVIDENCE:

When Hamlet is displaced in his mother's affections by his uncle, he experiences a severe internal conflict over the question of whether or not to murder his uncle.

III. CONCLUSION

A. THESIS RESTATED IN A SLIGHTLY DIFFERENT WAY:

I conclude that Hamlet's internal conflict over whether or not to murder his uncle can be explained by Freud's theory of human sexuality.

B. DOES YOUR TOPIC QUESTION REQUIRE YOU TO DEVELOP A NEW SOLUTION TO A PROBLEM?

Often, your topic question requires you to develop a new solution that explains a set of facts. Your solution takes the form of a theory, or a *generalization*. In this case, you want to use *inductive reasoning*.

EXAMPLE:

TOPIC QUESTION:

What [generalization] explains [a given set of facts]?

EXAMPLE:

What [circumstances] explain [Rembrandt's use of light and shadow in his early paintings]?

ANALYSIS USING INDUCTIVE REASONING:

SPECIFIC FACTS:

I examine [a given set of facts].

EXAMPLE:

I examine [Rembrandt's use of light and shadow in his painting, *The Money Changer* (1627)].

I examine [Rembrandt's use of light and shadow in his painting, *St. Paul Seated in Contemplation* (c. 1629–30)].

I examine [Rembrandt's use of light and shadow in his painting, *Presentation in the Temple* (1631)].

COMMON CHARACTERISTICS:

I identify the characteristics that are common to [a given set of facts].

EXAMPLE:

I find [that, in each painting, Rembrandt's use of light and shadow makes individual figures stand out against a dark background].

I find [that, in each painting, Rembrandt's use of light and shadow highlights facial expressions].

I find [that, in each painting, Rembrandt's use of light and shadow creates a sense of drama].

CONCLUSION (INFERENCE):

I make a generalization based on the facts that I have observed.

EXAMPLE:

I make the following generalization based on the pictures that I have viewed: Rembrandt used light and shadow to convey a high level of emotional intensity.

FROM ANALYSIS TO ARGUMENT:

Note that the organization of the analysis has been turned upside-down.

I. INTRODUCTION

    A. TOPIC QUESTION:

        How do we explain Rembrandt's use of light and shadow in his early paintings?

    B. THESIS STATEMENT:

        Rembrandt used light and shadow to convey a high level of emotional intensity in his early works.

II. DISCUSSION

    A. POINT 1:

        Rembrandt used light and shadow to make individual figures stand out against a dark background, a technique that increased the emotional intensity of the work.

        1. EVIDENCE:

            The use of light and shadow in *The Presentation in the Temple* (1631).

B. Point 2:

Rembrandt used light and shadow to highlight facial expressions, particularly those that expressed powerful emotions.

1. Evidence:

The use of light and shadow in *St. Paul Seated in Contemplation* (c. 1629–30).

C. Point 3:

Rembrandt used light and shadow to create a sense of drama that evokes an emotional response in the viewer.

1. Evidence:

The use of light and shadow in *The Money Changer* (1627).

III. CONCLUSION

A. Thesis restated in a slightly different way:

Rembrandt's use of light and shadow allowed him to create an emotional intensity in his early paintings that was not present in his later work.

C. DOES YOUR TOPIC QUESTION REQUIRE YOU TO FOCUS ON THE *DEFINITION* OF A WORD, TERM, OR CONCEPT?

If your topic question requires you to define a word, term, or concept, you use *inductive reasoning*. In this case, your definition takes the form of a judgment, or a generalization.

EXAMPLE:

Topic question:

How do I define [a given word, term, or concept]?

EXAMPLE:

How do I define "courage"?

Analysis using inductive reasoning:

Specific facts:

I list specific examples that characterize [a given word, term, or concept].

EXAMPLE:

Rescue workers showed courage when they rushed into the burning department store to save shoppers trapped by fire.

The owner of the corner deli showed courage when he ran into traffic to save a child who had wandered into the street.

COMMON CHARACTERISTICS:

I note that these specific examples share several common characteristics.

EXAMPLE:

In both instances, those who showed courage helped other people out of potentially disastrous situations.

In both instances, those who showed courage acted without regard to their personal safety.

CONCLUSION (INFERENCE):

I conclude by suggesting that [a given word, term, or concept] is best defined by [my generalization].

EXAMPLE:

I believe that [courage] is best defined as [the willingness to help others without considering one's own personal safety].

FROM ANALYSIS TO ARGUMENT:

Note that the organization of the analysis has been turned upside-down.

I. INTRODUCTION

   A. TOPIC QUESTION:

   How do I define "courage"?

   B. THESIS STATEMENT:

   I believe that courage is best defined as the willingness to help others without considering one's personal safety.

II. DISCUSSION

   A. POINT 1:

   Courageous people help others out of potentially dangerous situations.

     1. EVIDENCE.

     Rescue workers showed courage when they rushed into the burning department store to save shoppers trapped by fire.

   B. POINT 2:

   Courageous people act without regard to their personal safety.

1. EVIDENCE.

The owner of the corner deli showed courage when he ran into traffic to save a child who had wandered into the street.

III. CONCLUSION

A. THESIS RESTATED IN A SLIGHTLY DIFFERENT WAY:

These examples support my belief that courage is best defined as the willingness to aid others without considering the personal cost.

D. DOES YOUR TOPIC QUESTION REQUIRE YOU TO FOCUS ON THE *DESCRIPTION* OF A PERSON, PLACE, THING, OR SITUATION TO LEAVE THE READER WITH A DOMINANT IMPRESSION?

Descriptive essays allow you to use sense impressions (sight, sound, touch, taste, and smell) to express your judgment about a person, place, thing, or situation. If your topic question requires you to use description, you use *inductive reasoning*.

EXAMPLE:

TOPIC QUESTION:

How do I describe [a person, place, thing, or situation]?

EXAMPLE:

How do I describe a summer day at the beach?

ANALYSIS USING INDUCTIVE REASONING:

SPECIFIC FACTS:

I list specific examples that characterize [a person, place, thing, or situation].

EXAMPLE:

I describe children in bright pink bathing suits playing on the sand.

I describe the cries of the seagulls as they swoop from the clifftops and dive to devour the remains of picnic lunches left on the sand.

I describe the smell of suntan oil and the sound of the surf crashing on the shore.

COMMON CHARACTERISTICS:

My examples suggest [a person, place, thing, or situation].

EXAMPLE:

My examples suggest [that it is a hot and sunny day, since the children wear swim suits and suntan oil].

My examples suggest [that it is late in the day since the picnic lunches are left on the sand for the gulls to eat].

My examples also suggest [that it is a good day for being at the beach].

CONCLUSION (INFERENCE):

I conclude by suggesting that [a person, place, thing, or situation] is best described by [my generalization]. I make the following generalization based on the examples I have chosen:

EXAMPLE:

The perfect day on the beach is long, hot, and sun-soaked.

FROM ANALYSIS TO ARGUMENT:

I. INTRODUCTION

   A. TOPIC QUESTION:

       How do I describe a summer day at the beach?

   B. THESIS STATEMENT:

       It was a perfect day. Long, hot, and sun-soaked.

II. DISCUSSION

   A. EVIDENCE.

       Children in bright pink bathing suits played on the sand.

   B. EVIDENCE.

       Overhead, seagulls swooped and screamed as they dived to devour the remains of picnic lunches left on the sand.

   C. EVIDENCE.

       I sat and soaked in the atmosphere: the smell of suntan oil and the sound of the surf crashing on the shore.

III. CONCLUSION

   A. THESIS RESTATED IN A SLIGHTLY DIFFERENT WAY:

       At that moment in time, there was no place I would rather be.

E. **DOES YOUR TOPIC QUESTION REQUIRE YOU TO FOCUS ON THE *COMPARISON* OF SOME ASPECT OF A PERSON, PLACE, THING, OR IDEA WITH ANOTHER SIMILARLY SITUATED TO DEMONSTRATE THEIR RELATIONSHIP?**

The goal of comparison questions is to make a generalization about the relationship between two related concepts. To do that, you need to choose one or more points of comparison.

Topic question:

How is [a person, place, thing, or idea] similar to or different from [another person, place, thing, or idea]?

EXAMPLE:

How are entering freshmen students at the University of Chicago similar to, or different from, entering freshmen students at Columbia University?

Analysis:

Points of comparison:

I choose one or more points of comparison.

EXAMPLE:

I compare entering freshmen students at the University of Chicago and at Columbia University using the following points of comparison: SAT scores, geographic distribution, and type of secondary school attended.

Compare and contrast:

I compare and contrast [a person, place, thing, or idea] with [another person, place, thing, or idea] using my points of comparison.

EXAMPLE:

I compare [freshmen students at University of Chicago] with those at Columbia University] on the basis of [their SAT scores].

I compare [freshmen students at University of Chicago] with [those at Columbia University] on the basis of [their geographic origins].

I compare [freshmen students at University of Chicago] with [those at Columbia University] on the basis of [the type of secondary school that they attended].

Conclusion (inference):

I make a generalization based on my analysis of the relationship between two related [aspects of a person, place, thing, or idea].

EXAMPLE:

I find that entering freshmen at the University of Chicago are similar to those at Columbia University on the basis of SAT scores, geographic distribution, and type of secondary school attended. I conclude that the University of Chicago and Columbia University admit very similar entering classes.

You can arrange your argument in one of two ways.

1. FROM ANALYSIS TO ARGUMENT 1: This is the first method.
   I. INTRODUCTION
      A. TOPIC QUESTION:

      How do entering freshmen students at the University of Chicago compare with entering freshmen students at Columbia University?

      B. THESIS STATEMENT:

      My comparison of the freshmen at the University of Chicago and Columbia University shows that these two schools admit very similar entering classes.

   II. DISCUSSION
      A. SAMPLE #1:

      Freshmen at the University of Chicago
         1. FIRST POINT OF COMPARISON: SAT scores
         2. SECOND POINT OF COMPARISON: Geographic distribution
         3. THIRD POINT OF COMPARISON: Type of secondary school attended

      B. SAMPLE #2:

      Freshmen at Columbia University
         1. FIRST POINT OF COMPARISON: SAT scores
         2. SECOND POINT OF COMPARISON: Geographic distribution
         3. THIRD POINT OF COMPARISON: Type of secondary school attended

   III. CONCLUSION
      A. THESIS RESTATED IN A SLIGHTLY DIFFERENT WAY:

      Freshmen entering the University of Chicago and Columbia University share many of the same characteristics.

2. FROM ANALYSIS TO ARGUMENT 2: This is the second way to organize your argument.
   I. INTRODUCTION
      A. TOPIC QUESTION:

      How do entering freshmen at the University of Chicago compare with entering freshmen at Columbia University?

B. Thesis statement:

My comparison of the freshmen at the University of Chicago and at Columbia University shows that these two schools admit very similar entering classes.

II. DISCUSSION

    A. First point of comparison: SAT scores

        1. Sample 1: Freshmen at the University of Chicago

        2. Sample 2: Freshmen at Columbia University

    B. Second point of comparison: Geographic distribution

        1. Sample 1: Freshmen at the University of Chicago

        2. Sample 2: Freshmen at Columbia University

    C. Third point of comparison: Type of secondary school attended

        1. Sample 1: Freshmen at the University of Chicago

        2. Sample 2: Freshmen at Columbia University

III. CONCLUSION

    A. Thesis restated in a slightly different way:

Freshmen entering the University of Chicago and Columbia University share many of the same characteristics.

III. Checklist

A. **DEVELOP YOUR ANALYSIS USING *DEDUCTIVE REASONING* IF YOUR TOPIC QUESTION REQUIRES YOU TO:**

Apply existing knowledge to a given body of information.

B. **DEVELOP YOUR ANALYSIS USING *INDUCTIVE REASONING* IF YOUR TOPIC QUESTION REQUIRES YOU TO:**

1. Develop a new solution to a problem.

2. Focus on the definition of a word, term, or concept.

3. Focus on the description of a person, place, thing, or situation to leave the reader with a dominant impression.

4. Focus on the comparison of some aspect of a person, place, thing, or idea with another similarly situated.

Part III

PLAN YOUR WRITING STRATEGY

An academic essay is assigned to enable a student to learn three things:

1. How to explore a subject area and to make a judgment about a particular issue.
2. How to create an argument supporting that judgment using reasoning and evidence.
3. **How to write an interesting and coherently organized essay.**

Many students consider the actual writing of a research paper to be the hardest part of the learning process. Almost everyone has experienced "writer's panic" or "writer's block." These problems are almost invariably caused by an attempt to put words on paper before you have actually thought out and organized your ideas.

If you follow the guidelines presented in the first two parts of this book, you may never experience "writer's block" again. By the time you begin to write coherent sentences, you should already have a thesis statement, an organizational pattern, and a body of coherent evidence.

This final section focuses on the strategy, craft, and presentation of the academic essay. Chapter 7 describes the most effective way of presenting information about your topic to the reader. Chapter 8 shows you how to evaluate your written work and to improve your use of basic tools such as words, sentences, and paragraphs. Chapter 9 evaluates the essay as a whole and suggests ways that you can improve its style and presentation.

How to Plan Your Writing Strategy

Once you have gathered the various elements of your argument, you can begin the next and final stage of your essay: the actual writing. As we suggested earlier, this should be the last thing you consider, not the first. In this chapter, we describe the four most important components of the essay: the introduction, the thesis paragraph, the discussion, and the conclusion. We also suggest ways to make your essay as interesting and persuasive as possible.

I. The Introduction

The purpose of the *introduction* is to attract your readers' interest and to lead them to your topic question. A good introduction lets your readers know that you do not intend to bore them, but will try to make your essay lively and interesting.

A. THERE ARE TWO TYPES OF INTRODUCTIONS.

1. A *FUNNEL* INTRODUCTION BEGINS WITH A BROAD, GENERAL SUBJECT AND NARROWS TO A SPECIFIC TOPIC. IT THEN INTRODUCES YOUR THESIS QUESTION OR YOUR THESIS STATEMENT.

EXAMPLE:

TOPIC QUESTION:

Why should John Pike be included among the great illustrators?

FUNNEL INTRODUCTION LEADING TO THE TOPIC QUESTION:

Over the past decade, many early twentieth-century artists have received renewed acclaim as participants in the "great age of illustration." Some of the best artists, however, have been overlooked by both museums and publishers. One artist in particular, John Pike, is known only to those who purchase his old-fashioned instruction books. However, I believe that Pike remains one of the great illustrators of his generation.

2. A *HOOK* IS A STARTLING IDEA THAT ATTRACTS YOUR READERS. "Hooked" like a fish to your bright idea and held by your "line," they read on. You can use a number of types of hooks:

   a. Tell an anecdote that illustrates your thesis statement.

   b. Use a quotation that illustrates your thesis statement.

      (1) The quotation may be from a figure who is central to your essay.

      (2) The quotation may be from an authority in the field.

   c. Make a controversial statement of opinion that leads directly to your thesis statement.

   d. Present a startling fact or statistic.

   e. Define an unusual term that is crucial to your topic.

   f. Refer to a current event.

   g. If your topic question is particularly startling or thought-provoking, you may use it as a hook.

EXAMPLE:

DRAMATIC (AND HIGHLY CONTROVERSIAL) HOOK FOR A RESEARCH PAPER OF OVER SIX PAGES IN LENGTH:

Fifteen minutes past eight in the morning, August 6, 1945. Hiroshima, Japan. A bright flash engulfed the city. In the blink of an eye a city was gone from the face of the earth and with it nearly 130,000 people. Three days later, another city, Nagasaki was also obliterated, killing over 40,000 people. Japan surrendered three weeks later, ending the Second World War.

For the last fifty years, we have been taught that the A-bombs dropped on Hiroshima and Nagasaki saved up to one million American lives that would have been lost if the United States had invaded Japan. Is this true? Was the bombing necessary? I believe that the answer is no. Recently released evidence suggests that a diplomatic solution could have been found, particularly as Japan was close to surrendering in the summer of 1945. Instead, the president and his advisors succumbed to anti-Japanese rhetoric and unleashed weapons of mass destruction on the world.

B. BEWARE OF THE "DEADLY INTRODUCTION."

This promises to bore your reader to death.

1. Avoid stating a platitude or a cliché.

WRONG: STATEMENT OF A PLATITUDE OR CLICHÉ.

It is often said that the squeaky wheel gets the grease. This implies that activists who can make their voices heard on both television and the airwaves necessarily dominate the political debate. My contention, however, is that even the most vocal activists cannot set the political agenda unless the majority of the American people want to hear what they have to say.

CORRECT: REFER TO A CURRENT EVENT.

A recent editorial in the *Hometown Courier* warned that highly vocal interest groups such as the Committee for Environmental Action have used their access to public television and radio to persuade voters to pass controversial ballot initiatives. This implies that media-savvy activists necessarily dominate any political debate. My contention, however, is that even the most vocal groups cannot set the political agenda unless the majority of the American people want to hear what they have to say.

2. Avoid using a dictionary definition of a word whose meaning is well understood.

WRONG: DICTIONARY DEFINITION OF WELL-KNOWN WORD.

The *Oxford American Dictionary* defines a relic as "something that survives from an earlier age." This is how I would describe my grandfather. He grew up during the Great Depression and he does not seem to realize that times have changed. For example, he is always warning me that, if I leave my job, I might not find another one. It makes me think that people who experience economic insecurity as young adults tend to avoid risk, particularly as they get older.

CORRECT: AN ANECDOTE THAT ILLUSTRATES YOUR THESIS STATEMENT.

"You are not going to leave your job," Grandfather asked, gazing at me as if expecting some kind of confirmation. We were seated in the kitchenette of his third-floor Brooklyn apartment, drinking tea from chipped china mugs. I nodded my head. "You'll never get another one, you know," he said.

My grandfather's attitude toward job security was formed during the Great Depression when many young men and women found it difficult to find work. Despite the fact that he now lives in an era of rapid economic expansion, he still has not come to terms with this new age. This suggests that people who experience economic insecurity as young adults tend to avoid risk, particularly as they get older.

3. Avoid a restatement of the assignment—"In this paper I propose to ...." Do not tell your readers what you plan to do. Show them.

EXAMPLE:

WRONG: RESTATEMENT OF THE ASSIGNMENT.

In this paper, I am going to show how artists and writers enhanced the personal authority of King Louis XIV (r. 1643–1715) after a period of massive political instability. I will focus on the construction of Louis XIV's palace at Versailles and on the fabrication of his image as Sun King. First, I will talk about how the palace came to be built. Then I will discuss the ways in which images of the sun were incorporated into the overall design.

CORRECT: A QUOTATION THAT ILLUSTRATES YOUR THESIS STATEMENT.

Versailles, the royal palace of King Louis XIV (r. 1643–1715), was known by contemporaries as "the palace of the sun." Here, writers and artists created the theatrical spectacles and visual images that enhanced the personal authority of the French king. Their aim was to show how Louis XIV had brought peace and stability to a country formerly wracked by religious civil war and political strife.

4. Avoid a pivoting sentence or paragraph.

EXAMPLE:

Although ..., nevertheless....

..., however, ...

While it is well known that ..., it is less well known that ....

EXAMPLE:

WRONG: PIVOTING PARAGRAPH.

It is well-known that economic stability helps to hold a marriage and a family together. As Charles L. Schottland puts it, "the possession of money by the American family means more than the ability to purchase goods and services. Money symbolizes security—economic, social and emotional security." What is less well-known is that welfare programs designed to subsidize income often have an adverse effect on family structure, particularly in the black community. My contention is that the reform of the current welfare system will help to stabilize the black family.

CORRECT: CONTROVERSIAL STATEMENT OF OPINION.

Money is destroying the black family. Welfare programs designed to subsidize income force unmarried men and women to live in separate households in order to receive benefits. This undermines the basic structure of family life. My contention is that the reform of the current welfare system will help to stabilize the black family by forcing men and women to share economic responsibilities. The result should be a decrease in both poverty and illegitimacy.

C. **THE LENGTH OF AN INTRODUCTION SHOULD BE RELATED TO THE NUMBER OF PAGES THAT YOU HAVE BEEN ASSIGNED TO WRITE.**

　1. For a short paper (one to six pages), you should limit your introduction to one or two sentences.

　2. For a longer paper (six or more pages), you may use an introduction which is as long as one paragraph in length.

II. The Thesis Paragraph

The thesis paragraph is often the most difficult part of the essay to write because it requires you to fit a considerable amount of information in a relatively small space. Although there is no shortcut to a good thesis paragraph, we believe that the following patterns make the writing process a little easier.

A. **THE BASIC THESIS PARAGRAPH INCLUDES AN INTRODUCTION, A THESIS STATEMENT, AND A BRIEF DESCRIPTION OF THE POINTS THAT WILL BE DISCUSSED.**

　1. IN A SHORT ESSAY (one to six pages), the introduction and thesis are combined into a single paragraph. Because you are writing a very short paper, you do not need to describe the points that you are going to discuss in the course of your essay. Your reader will discover them soon enough.

EXAMPLE:

PARAGRAPH I: Introduction and thesis paragraph

　SENTENCE 1: Introduction (one to two sentences)

Sᴇɴᴛᴇɴᴄᴇ 2: Topic question (transition sentence)

The main issue is whether....

Sᴇɴᴛᴇɴᴄᴇ 3: Thesis statement

I believe, based on the evidence I have found, that....

In 1692, a group of "witches" from Salem, Massachusetts, were brought before magistrates and charged with subverting and undermining "God's law." What was this law? Was it simply a set of rules designed to guide men's behavior? Or was the definition of law more complex, connected in some way with the norms and values of society itself? I believe that the law, expressed through the institutions of the court, acted as an ideology that reflected the values of the Salem village community.

2. Iɴ ᴀ ʟᴏɴɢᴇʀ ᴇssᴀʏ (six or more pages), the introduction and the thesis statement are contained in separate paragraphs. In this case, you need to mention the main points that you intend to discuss in your essay.

EXAMPLE:

Pᴀʀᴀɢʀᴀᴘʜ I: Introduction (three to five sentences)

Pᴀʀᴀɢʀᴀᴘʜ II: Thesis paragraph

Sᴇɴᴛᴇɴᴄᴇ 1: Topic question (transition)

The main issue is whether....

Sᴇɴᴛᴇɴᴄᴇ 2: Thesis statement

I believe, based on the evidence I have found, that....

Sᴇɴᴛᴇɴᴄᴇ 3: Statement of the main points

I will establish the following points, (1) ..., (2) ..., (3)....

In 1692, a group of "witches" from Salem, Massachusetts, were brought before magistrates and charged with subverting and undermining "God's law." According to their accusers, these men and women had acted under the direction of Satan to bring division and discord to the village. Sarah Good had railed against the magistrates, using "base and abusive words"; others had questioned the authority of village leaders. For this, and for other alleged misdeeds, they were condemned to die.

What did "God's law" mean to the colonists of seventeenth-century Salem? Was it simply a set of rules designed to guide men's behavior? Or was the definition of law more complex, connected in some way with the norms and values of society itself? I believe that the law, expressed through the institutions of the court, acted as an ideology that reflected the values of the Salem village community. This essay examines the role of the law in seventeenth-century society, and it shows how community sanctions were used to buttress the authority of "Christ's kingdom on earth."

B. A MORE DETAILED THESIS PARAGRAPH MAY ALSO INCLUDE A DISCUSSION OF THE IMPORTANCE OF YOUR TOPIC.

Often, you will find it necessary to explain to your reader why your choice of topic is important and/or relevant at this time. This is particularly important when a topic has been either badly overworked or overlooked as unimportant. You should locate this explanation at the beginning of your paper, preferably in one of the first few paragraphs.

1. IN A SHORT ESSAY (one to six pages), you can briefly mention your topic's importance after you state your topic question.

EXAMPLE:

PARAGRAPH I: Introduction and thesis paragraph

SENTENCE 1: Introduction (one to two sentences)

SENTENCE 2: Topic question (transition)

The main issue is whether....

SENTENCE 3: Importance of the topic (one sentence)

a. This topic is particularly important now because....

b. Despite extensive treatment of [this topic], I believe it is an issue that merits reconsideration.

c. This topic, which has been overlooked in the past, is important because....

SENTENCE 4: Thesis statement

I believe, based on the evidence I have found, that....

For over three hundred years, scholars have considered John Locke's *Two Treatises of Government* to be the most authoritative work on private property and the role of government. However, the question remains, what did Locke mean by "property"? This is particularly important in light of recent Supreme Court decisions that hinge on the definition of the term. In my opinion, Locke used "property" to mean more than land and possessions. He used it to secure an individual's right to his or her own person: body, mind, and soul.

2. IN A LONG ESSAY (six or more pages), you can describe the importance of your topic in a separate paragraph that follows your thesis and your description of main points.

EXAMPLE:
PARAGRAPH I: Introduction

PARAGRAPH II: Thesis paragraph

PARAGRAPH III: Importance of topic (extended)

  a. This topic is particularly important now because....

  b. Despite extensive treatment of [this topic], I believe it is an issue which merits reconsideration.

  c. This topic, which has been overlooked in the past, is important because....

C. **A MORE DETAILED SET OF INTRODUCTORY PARAGRAPHS MAY ALSO CONTAIN INFORMATION ON THE ORIGIN AND HISTORY OF THE TOPIC.**

In some cases, your reader needs to know the history and/or origin of your topic question to appreciate your contribution. If you feel that you need to include this information, place it in a separate paragraph, close to the beginning of your essay.

  1. IN A LONG ESSAY (six or more pages), the *history* of a topic is contained in a separate paragraph that follows your thesis and your description of the topic's importance.

EXAMPLE:
PARAGRAPH I: Introduction

PARAGRAPH II: Thesis paragraph

  SENTENCE 1: Topic question (transition)

  The main issue is whether....

  SENTENCE 2: Thesis statement

  I believe, based on the evidence I have found, that....

  SENTENCE 3: Statement of the main points

  I will establish the following points, (1) ..., (2) ..., (3)....

PARAGRAPH III: Importance of the topic

PARAGRAPH IV: Origin and history of the topic

It is important to understand how this topic has been regarded in the past.

(1) When a topic is important *because of its history,* paragraphs III and IV may be combined.

D. A MORE DETAILED SET OF INTRODUCTORY PARAGRAPHS MAY ALSO CONTAIN THE DEFINITION OF A CRUCIAL WORD OR PHRASE.

Sometimes the definition of a word or phrase is crucial to your argument. If this is the case, you need to define that term in a separate paragraph.

EXAMPLE:

PARAGRAPH I: Introduction

PARAGRAPH II: Thesis paragraph

    SENTENCE 1: Topic question (transition)

    The main issue is whether....

    SENTENCE 2: Thesis statement

    I believe, based on the evidence I have found, that....

    SENTENCE 3: Statement of the main points

    I will establish the following points, (1) ..., (2) ..., (3)....

PARAGRAPH III: Definition of terms

For the purposes of this paper, I use [a given word or phrase] to mean....

PARAGRAPH IV: Importance of the topic

PARAGRAPH V: Origin and history of the topic

E. A MORE DETAILED SET OF INTRODUCTORY PARAGRAPHS MAY ALSO CONTAIN A RESPONSE TO ANY ANTICIPATED OPPOSITION TO YOUR THESIS.

If your thesis is controversial, you might want to anticipate opposition to your point of view. You might choose to acknowledge persons who are likely to disagree with your thesis, describing their viewpoints in a single paragraph. Or you might choose to focus your entire paper on the controversy. In either case, you must inform your readers about the disagreement, and you must explain why your point of view is the correct one.

1. IN A SHORT ESSAY (one to six pages), acknowledge the opposing points of view in the thesis paragraph.

EXAMPLE:

PARAGRAPH I: Introduction and thesis paragraph

    SENTENCE 1: Introduction

    SENTENCE 2: Topic question

    SENTENCE 3: Acknowledge the opposing points of view

There are those who believe .... However, I believe that they are mistaken because....

    SENTENCE 4: Thesis statement

  2. IN A LONG ESSAY (six or more pages), acknowledge the opposing points of view in a separate paragraph.

EXAMPLE:

PARAGRAPH I: Introduction

PARAGRAPH II: Thesis paragraph

    SENTENCE 1: Topic question (transition)

The main issue is whether....

    SENTENCE 2: Thesis statement

I believe, based on the evidence I have found, that....

    SENTENCE 3: Statement of the main points

I will establish the following points, (1) ..., (2) ..., (3)....

PARAGRAPH III: Acknowledge the opposing points of view

There are those who believe .... *However, I believe that they are mistaken because....*

III. The Discussion

The purpose of the *discussion*, otherwise known as the body of your paper, is to prove to your readers that your judgment is correct. Here you present a series of points (or paragraphs) that support your thesis statement. In general, the structure of the discussion is far less complicated than that of the introduction.

A. HOW LONG SHOULD THE DISCUSSION BE?

First, consider the amount of space that you have to work with. In most cases, your discussion should take up one-half to two-thirds of the paper's length. The other one-half to one-third of the paper should be devoted to the introduction and conclusion. Once you decide how many pages you are going to write, you can figure out how much material to include in each of your paragraphs.

If you are going to write a four-page paper (1,000 words), your thesis paragraph and conclusion should each comprise no more than one-half of a page (125 words). The body of the paper should be approximately three pages in length. If you use three paragraphs for the body, you need enough material to fill one page (250 words) for each paragraph.

PAGE REQUIREMENT: 4 pages (1,000 words)

INTRODUCTION/THESIS PARAGRAPH: One-half page (125 words)

DISCUSSION: Three pages (750 words)

EACH PARAGRAPH: One page (250 words)

CONCLUSION: One-half page (125 words)

B. HOW MANY PARAGRAPHS SHOULD I USE?

Limit the number of paragraphs to ones that you can develop in the time and space available.

1. FOR SHORT ESSAYS (one to six pages), limit yourself to three or four paragraphs.

2. FOR LONGER ESSAYS (six or more pages), you may limit yourself to three main points and develop these points more fully than you would in a shorter paper. In this case, you might want to support each point with one or more paragraphs.

C. FOR INFORMATION ON THE USE OF EVIDENCE, SEE CHAPTER 4.

D. FOR INFORMATION ON PARAGRAPH STRUCTURE, SEE CHAPTER 8.

E. MAKE SURE THAT YOUR PARAGRAPHS REMAIN CLEAR AND EASY TO FOLLOW.

1. Avoid generalizations. Instead, use specific facts, such as proper names and dates.

GENERALIZATION:

A senator has said that government expenditures could be cut during the current fiscal year.

BETTER, MORE SPECIFIC, STATEMENT:

Senator Boll Weevil (D–Georgia) suggested that government expenditures could be cut by 20% during the fiscal year 1998 by eliminating the CIA.

2. Limit anecdotes and descriptions to one paragraph to keep them from overwhelming your other evidence.

3. Avoid block quotes—lengthy passages that take up more than three lines—since readers tend to ignore them. Instead, paraphrase a long passage in your own words.

4. Avoid excessive quotation. Numerous quotes break up the flow of your writing and can confuse your reader. Use your own words whenever possible.

5. Make sure that you describe the source of your quote, either in the body of your essay or in a footnote.

EXAMPLE:

WRONG:

It has been suggested that "stability became the crucial prerequisite to slow and orderly change in the eighteenth century."

CORRECT:

J. H. Plumb in his book, *The Growth of Political Stability,* suggested that "stability became the crucial prerequisite to slow and orderly change in the eighteenth century."

CORRECT:

One expert has suggested that "stability became the crucial prerequisite to slow and orderly change in the eighteenth century."[2]

IV. The Conclusion

The purpose of the *conclusion* is to summarize the main points made in the discussion and to assert that these points, taken cumulatively, prove your thesis statement. The conclusion

---

[2]J. H. Plumb, *The Growth of Political Stability* (1967).

should not only give your reader a sense of completion, but it should also provide a final dramatic statement.

A. HOW LONG SHOULD THE CONCLUSION BE?

Again, your conclusion should be no longer than your introduction and thesis statement.

1. IN A SHORT ESSAY (one to six pages), the conclusion should consist of a single paragraph. It should be no longer than half a page in length.

2. IN A LONG ESSAY (six or more pages), your conclusion may consist of one or more paragraphs.

B. WHAT ARE THE BEST WAYS TO CONCLUDE THE ESSAY?

1. You may refer the reader back to a question that you posed in the introduction.

EXAMPLE:

What did "God's law" mean to the inhabitants of Salem? As we have seen, it was more than the set of rules found in the Old and New Testaments. It also referred to a set of moral injunctions that expressed the values of the community as a whole. This broader definition of "God's law" allowed Salem villagers to bring charges of witchcraft before a secular magistrate. It also made it possible for them to define the nature of civil society itself.

2. You may comment on the possible significance of your thesis statement for the present or for the future.

EXAMPLE:

Locke's definition of the term "property" is crucial to our understanding of the current legal debates over the original intent of the United States Constitution. It requires us to conclude that the right to privacy is protected under both the fourth and fifth amendments of the Bill of Rights. It also suggests that controversial Supreme Court decisions, such as *Roe v. Wade* (1973), are more constitutional than opponents may hope and supporters may think.

3. You may use a significant example, anecdote, or quotation. If necessary, take a piece of evidence from the body of your paper and use it in the conclusion to increase its dramatic impact.

The illegitimacy rate among blacks was 48 percent in 1980, up from 23 percent in 1963. Clearly, this is the result of welfare policies that keep men and women from marrying and forming a coherent family unit. It is my hope that a reformed welfare policy will reduce the numbers of illegitimate births and restore the integrity of the black family.

C. WHAT ARE THE WORST WAYS TO CONCLUDE THE ESSAY?

1. Do not restate your thesis statement with as much drama as possible.

2. Do not start on a completely new topic.

3. Do not pretend to have proven more than you have.

4. Do not apologize or bring your thesis into doubt.

V. Checklist: The Elements of an Argument

A. IN THE INTRODUCTION AND THESIS PARAGRAPH YOU STATE:

I believe [thesis statement]. My thesis is true because [point A, point B, and point C].

B. IN THE DISCUSSION YOU STATE:

My thesis statement is true because I can *prove* my points, A, B, and C are true and related to my thesis statement.

1. Point A is true because I can provide items of evidence 1, 2, 3.

2. Point B is true because I can provide items of evidence 4, 5, 6.

3. Point C is true because I can provide items of evidence 7, 8, 9.

I have proven that point A is true, point B is true and point C is true. Therefore, my thesis statement must be true.

Chapter 8

How to Improve Your Writing Style

Good essays are written in a clear and accessible style. You want your readers to be able to understand and appreciate your argument without becoming distracted by misused words, faulty sentences, or poor paragraph structure.

In this chapter, we offer a few basic tips to help you improve your writing style. If you need additional assistance with these ideas, consult your teacher or a librarian for other published works on the subject.

Good writing is not a matter of talent or luck. It is hard work. If you really want to be a *good* writer, practice writing every day.

I. Paragraph Structure

A. A PARAGRAPH IS A *SHORT ARGUMENT* THAT SUPPORTS ONE MAIN IDEA ABOUT YOUR TOPIC.

B. FOUR TYPES OF SENTENCES MAKE UP A PARAGRAPH.

1. THE TOPIC SENTENCE is a general statement, or argument, that you intend to prove in the body of the paragraph.

   a. It states one *main idea* about your topic, the idea discussed in the body of the paragraph.

   b. Every other sentence in the paragraph must be related and subordinate to the topic sentence.

2. A SUPPORTING SENTENCE backs up the assertion made in your topic sentence. The paragraph may contain as many supporting sentences as you wish.

3. A LIMITING SENTENCE reduces the scope of the topic sentence in some way. There should be only one limiting sentence per paragraph.

4. A TRANSITIONAL SENTENCE links paragraphs with a common idea. It is always the last sentence in a direct paragraph.

C. THERE ARE THREE BASIC TYPES OF PARAGRAPHS.

1. In a DIRECT PARAGRAPH, the first sentence is a topic sentence. The topic sentence is then followed by either supporting sentences or by a limiting sentence.

EXAMPLE:

DIRECT PARAGRAPH:

The rise of the new physics has been accompanied by a tremendous growth of interest in the deeper philosophical implications of science. Over the past half-century, physicists have moved away from strictly mechanical models of the universe to a view that sees the mind as playing an integral role in all physical events. This has led many people to question assumptions about the origin and nature of the universe. Paul Davies, in *God and the New Physics* (1983), argues that the discovery that the mind exists "as an abstract, holistic, organizational pattern, capable of disembodiment, refutes the reductionist philosophy that we are all nothing but moving mounds of atoms." It has also raised the question whether the universe could have been conceived by an infinite mind, God.

TOPIC SENTENCE:

The rise of the new physics has been accompanied by a tremendous growth of interest in the deeper philosophical implications of science.

LIMITING SENTENCE:

Over the past half-century, physicists have moved away from strictly mechanical models of the universe to a view that sees the mind as playing an integral role in all physical events.

SUPPORTING SENTENCE:

This has led many people to question assumptions about the origin and nature of the universe.

SUPPORTING SENTENCE:

Paul Davies, in *God and the New Physics* (1983), argues that the discovery that the mind exists "as an abstract, holistic, organizational pattern, capable of disembodiment, refutes the reductionist philosophy that we are all nothing but moving mounds of atoms."

TRANSITION SENTENCE:

It has also raised the question whether the universe could have been conceived by an infinite mind, God.

2. In a PIVOTING PARAGRAPH the first sentence is a limiting sentence. The limiting sentence is often followed by a supporting sentence, a pivoting sentence, and, finally, the topic sentence.

  a. A PIVOTING SENTENCE turns the paragraph in a new direction. Such sentences often include the following words:

EXAMPLE:

Although ..., nevertheless ....

..., however, ...

While it is well known that ..., it is less well known that ....

EXAMPLE:

PIVOTING PARAGRAPH:

Science often is considered to be a system of thought that is incompatible with religious belief. After all, it was a biologist, Charles Darwin, who argued in *The Origin of the Species* that all living creatures evolved through the processes of mutation and natural selection, not through the intervention of an omnipotent God. In recent years, however, scientists, particularly physical scientists, have become more deeply religious than ever. New research into the origin and structure of the universe has led a number of prominent physicists to argue that God exists in the deep, rational beauty of the natural world.

LIMITING SENTENCE:

Science often is considered to be a system of thought that is incompatible with religious belief.

SUPPORTING SENTENCE:

After all, it was a biologist, Charles Darwin, who argued in *The Origin of the Species* that all living creatures evolved through the processes of mutation and natural selection, not through the intervention of an omnipotent God.

PIVOTING SENTENCE:

In recent years, however, scientists, particularly physical scientists, have become more deeply religious than ever.

TOPIC SENTENCE:

New research into the origin and structure of the universe has led a number of prominent physicists to argue that God exists in the deep, rational beauty of the natural world.

3. In a SUSPENDED PARAGRAPH, the topic sentence is placed at the end of the paragraph. Meanwhile, supporting and/or limiting sentences are used to build toward the topic sentence.

    a. Thesis paragraphs and concluding paragraphs are frequently suspended paragraphs.

EXAMPLE:

SUSPENDED PARAGRAPH:

Physical scientists often express the rational beauty of the natural world—its harmony, simplicity, and symmetry—through the language of mathematics. Paul Dirac, for example, once observed that "it is more important to have beauty in one's equations than to have them fit experiment," and John Wheeler wrote that "the beauty in the laws of physics is the fantastic simplicity that they have." I believe that it is through the creation of simple, elegant mathematical equations that physical scientists illustrate their belief in a divinely ordered universe and a rational God.

LIMITING SENTENCE:

Physical scientists often express the rational beauty of the natural world—its harmony, simplicity, and symmetry—through the language of mathematics.

SUPPORTING SENTENCE:

Paul Dirac, for example, once observed that "it is more important to have beauty in one's equations than to have them fit experiment," and John Wheeler wrote that "the beauty in the laws of physics is the fantastic simplicity that they have."

TOPIC SENTENCE:

I believe that it is through the creation of simple, elegant mathematical equations that physical scientists illustrate their belief in a divinely ordered universe and a rational God.

D. THE POSITION OF THE SENTENCES IN A PARAGRAPH IS IMPORTANT.

1. THE FIRST SENTENCE IS ALWAYS IN THE STRONGEST POSITION. The reader always looks to the first sentence to find the subject of your paragraph.

2. THE MIDDLE SENTENCES ARE IN THE WEAKEST POSITION. They are the most likely to be overlooked by the reader. If you put your topic sentence in the middle of the paragraph, your reader is sure to miss it.

3. THE LAST SENTENCE IS IN THE POSITION OF SECONDARY IMPORTANCE. While the last sentence does not have as strong a position as the first, it is still important. For example, in an anecdote, the last sentence is called the *punch line.*

E. THE ORDER OF IDEAS IN A PARAGRAPH IS IMPORTANT.

There are a number of possible orders:

1. GENERAL TO SPECIFIC. This involves using a generalization followed by a number of specific instances.

2. SPECIFIC TO GENERAL. This involves using a number of specific instances followed by a generalization.

3. MOST IMPORTANT TO LEAST IMPORTANT

4. MOST ACCESSIBLE TO LEAST ACCESSIBLE

5. THE MOST FAMILIAR TO THE LEAST FAMILIAR IDEA

6. THE GREATEST NUMBER TO THE FEWEST NUMBER

7. THE HIGHEST QUALITY TO THE LOWEST QUALITY

8. LARGEST SIZE TO SMALLEST SIZE

9. ORDERING BY NUMBER WITHOUT REFERENCE TO CHRONOLOGY

10. ORDERING BY TIME (OR CHRONOLOGY)

F. A PARAGRAPH MAY BE SHORT OR LONG.

The length of a paragraph may be as short as one or two sentences or as long as one page (250 words). The only rule is that it must be long enough to develop your main point adequately.

1. If your paragraph seems to be too long, begin a new paragraph.

2. Be sure to vary the lengths of your paragraphs. Try writing one long paragraph followed by one short paragraph and one medium-sized paragraph. Variation increases the dramatic effect of your writing and keeps your reader interested.

G. **IF YOU ARE HAVING TROUBLE WRITING A PARAGRAPH:**

   1. WRITE THE TOPIC SENTENCE OF THE PARAGRAPH FIRST. This ensures that you have an argument in mind before you begin to write the other sentences.

   2. USE ONLY ONE MAIN POINT PER PARAGRAPH. Do not let yourself be sidetracked by competing ideas.

   3. IF YOU MAKE A GENERALIZATION, IT MUST BE CONTAINED IN THE TOPIC SENTENCE. The other sentences either support or limit that generalization.

   4. ORGANIZE THE SEQUENCE OF SUPPORTING SENTENCES IN SOME KIND OF ORDER.

   5. DO NOT WORRY ABOUT TRANSITION SENTENCES IN YOUR FIRST DRAFT.

II. Sentence Structure

A. **A SENTENCE IS THE EXPRESSION OF AN IDEA ABOUT A SUBJECT.**

   1. The subject of our thought is the called *subject* of our sentence.

   2. What we think about that subject is called the *predicate.*

B. **THERE ARE THREE KINDS OF SENTENCES.**

   1. A SIMPLE SENTENCE is a single independent statement of fact. It contains a subject and a predicate along with a connecting verb.

      a. A simple sentence is easy to understand and easy to write.

      b. If we used only simple sentences in our writing, it would sound choppy and childlike. Each sentence would sound the same.

   2. A COMPOUND SENTENCE contains two (or more) simple sentences of equal importance joined by words like *and* and

or. When two sentences are joined, the first becomes stronger simply by reason of its position.

3. A COMPLEX SENTENCE consists of two (or more) separate statements joined by words like *but* and *however.* It may also contain phrases, starting with words such as *which, that, in, because,* etc.

C. TIPS ON WRITING GOOD SENTENCES:

1. PUT THE SUBJECT CLOSE TO THE BEGINNING OF A SENTENCE. Do not bury it behind a lengthy clause.

EXAMPLE:

SUBJECT BURIED BEHIND A LENGTH CLAUSE:

Despite efforts by the Dalai Lama and other Tibetan spiritual leaders to regain their homeland, the Chinese government is unwilling to grant independence to Tibet.

SUBJECT UP FRONT:

The Chinese government is unwilling to grant independence to Tibet, despite efforts by the Dalai Lama and other Tibetan spiritual leaders to regain their homeland.

2. USE THE ACTIVE TENSE RATHER THAN THE PASSIVE TENSE. Avoid using the verb forms *is, are, was, were* too often. The overuse of these verbs makes you sound as though you lack conviction and confidence in your ideas.

EXAMPLE:

PASSIVE TENSE:

It *was* in the fortified city of Lhasa, in Tibet, that the Dalai Lama lived.

ACTIVE TENSE:

The Dalai Lama *lived* in the fortified city of Lhasa in Tibet.

3. VARY THE LENGTH OF YOUR SENTENCES. For example, you might use one compound sentence followed by a simple sentence. By varying the lengths of your sentences, you make your writing much more interesting to read.

EXAMPLE:

SENTENCES ALL THE SAME LENGTH:

Tibet developed close ties with China in the eighteenth century. The Dalai Lama agreed to become the spiritual guide of the Manchu emperor. He accepted patronage and protection in return for advice. This relationship was the first formal tie between the Tibetans and the Qing Dynasty (1644–1911).

Varied sentence length:

Tibet developed close ties with eighteenth-century China when the Dalai Lama agreed to become the spiritual guide of the Manchu emperor. He accepted patronage and protection in return for advice. This relationship was the first formal tie between the Tibetans and the Qing Dynasty (1644–1911).

III. Word Usage

The use of inappropriate words or phrases can cause your reader to misunderstand your meaning. It can also undermine your credibility when you are trying to make a persuasive argument.

A. USE PLAIN WORDS FOR CRISP, INTERESTING WRITING.

If your readers do not understand your words, they will not try to understand your ideas. Remember, the most complex ideas can be expressed in simple language.

1. Use nouns that express specific, concrete ideas rather than abstract generalizations or judgments.

EXAMPLE:

Wrong: Nouns that express abstract generalizations.

Beethoven wrote a piece of music that was supposed to sound like a trip to the country.

Correct: Nouns that express specific, concrete ideas.

Beethoven's Symphony No. 6 (*Pastoral*) expressed the beauty and mystery of the Vienna countryside.

2. Use active rather than passive verbs.

EXAMPLE:

Wrong: Passive verb tense.

Heavy winds from the southwest *were brought* by spring storms.

Correct: Active verb tense.

Spring storms *brought* heavy winds from the southwest.

3. Use adjectives and adverbs only when they are absolutely necessary to convey meaning. In general, one adjective or adverb per sentence is more than enough.

WRONG: OVERUSE OF ADJECTIVES.

He saw grassy meadows covered by sweet, aromatic plants and grazed by hundreds of slow moving sheep.

CORRECT: MODERATE USE OF ADJECTIVES.

He saw grassy meadows grazed by hundreds of sheep.

4. Use simple language whenever possible.

WRONG: PRETENTIOUS LANGUAGE.

George is the most obstreperous infant that I have ever had the opportunity to meet.

CORRECT: SIMPLE LANGUAGE.

George is the noisiest child that I have ever met.

B. DEFINE OBSCURE WORDS OR TERMS.

EXAMPLE:

WRONG: OBSCURE TERM, UNDEFINED.

I plan to specialize in organology and to complete my Ph.D. research at Stanford.

CORRECT: OBSCURE TERM, DEFINED.

I plan to specialize in organology, the science dealing with the development of plant and animal organs, and to complete my Ph.D. research at Stanford.

C. USE WORDS CORRECTLY.

If you are unsure of the meaning of a word, look it up in the dictionary.

EXAMPLE:

WRONG: INCORRECT USE OF A WORD.

Raul began his *dissent* down the steep hillside.

CORRECT: CORRECT USE OF A WORD.

Raul began his *descent* down the steep hillside.

D. AVOID WORDS AND PHRASES THAT OBSCURE YOUR MEANING.

1. PREPACKAGED EXPRESSIONS, like frozen food, have a short "shelf life" and they are likely to be stale by the time that you use them.

   a. *Clichés* are expressions that have been used so often that they have become meaningless.

Wʀᴏɴɢ: Cʟɪᴄʜé.

My friend, Georgia, is pregnant and she is *as big as a house.*

Cᴏʀʀᴇᴄᴛ: Oʀɪɢɪɴᴀʟ ʟᴀɴɢᴜᴀɢᴇ.

My friend, Georgia, is pregnant and she looks uncomfortably large.

  b. *Jargon* is technical or professional language used out of context. The use of jargon tends to obscure your real meaning.

EXAMPLE:

Cᴏᴍᴘᴜᴛᴇʀᴇsᴇ, sᴇʟꜰ-ʜᴇʟᴘ ᴘsʏᴄʜᴏʟᴏɢᴇsᴇ:

  2. Uɴᴛʀᴀɴsʟᴀᴛᴇᴅ ᴡᴏʀᴅs ᴏʀ ᴘʜʀᴀsᴇs ɪɴ ᴀ ꜰᴏʀᴇɪɢɴ ʟᴀɴɢᴜᴀɢᴇ are effective barriers to communication. Always provide an English translation unless you are sure that readers will understand the meaning of the phrase.

EXAMPLE:

Wʀᴏɴɢ: Uɴᴛʀᴀɴsʟᴀᴛᴇᴅ ᴘʜʀᴀsᴇ.

Contemporaries described the palace of the Louvre as *toute la structure imprime le respect dans l'esprit des peuples.*

Cᴏʀʀᴇᴄᴛ: Tʀᴀɴsʟᴀᴛᴇᴅ ᴘʜʀᴀsᴇ.

Contemporaries described the palace of the Louvre as impressing respect on the peoples of the world [*toute la structure imprime le respect dans l'esprit des peuples*].

E. IF YOU WANT TO BE JUDGED SOLELY ON THE BASIS OF YOUR IDEAS, USE STANDARD WRITTEN ENGLISH.

Slang, clichés, mixed metaphors, and regional speech patterns are often hard for you to "hear" if you grew up with them. You understand their meaning and assume that everyone else does, too. However, you should avoid using nonstandard words or phrases in essays, particularly in academic essays, because your reader may not know what they mean. Furthermore, your use of certain words may allow others to identify you by your age, education, profession, sex, ethnic origin, and socioeconomic class. This identification may become a factor in your readers' willingness to listen to your ideas. This is why it is so important to use Standard Written English. If you are having problems identifying Standard Written English, here are some suggestions:

1. Listen to the television network newspeople. Many of them overcame serious language handicaps to become excellent readers of Standard Written English.

2. Ask your librarian for audiotapes of books with the accompanying text. Listen to the tapes and read aloud along with them. Try to hear the rhythm of the language as well as the sound of the words.

   a. The breathing places and pauses help you identify the natural divisions in a sentences. They are taken at the at the end of a sentence, at the beginning and end of a clause, and sometimes just before the verb.

   b. Listen to the words that the speaker emphasizes.

3. Copy down paragraphs or short essays that you think are particularly well-written. Note the length and structure of the sentences, the size and number of paragraphs used, and the types of words chosen. See if you can imitate this style in your own writing.

F. CHECK SPELLING AND WORD USAGE.

Problems with spelling and a limited vocabulary can be helped by using a dictionary and a thesaurus. Keep one of each on your desk for ready reference, and carry a small paperback version of one or the other to read when you are traveling by bus or train. You will be amazed at how much knowledge you can acquire in this way.

IV. Checklist

A. WRITE A TOPIC SENTENCE FOR EACH PARAGRAPH.

B. BE SURE THAT EACH PARAGRAPH HAS A COHERENT INTERNAL STRUCTURE.

C. VARY THE LENGTH OF YOUR PARAGRAPHS.

D. CHECK YOUR SENTENCE STRUCTURE.

E. VARY THE LENGTH OF YOUR SENTENCES.

F. USE PLAIN WORDS FOR CRISP, INTERESTING WRITING.

G. USE STANDARD WRITTEN ENGLISH.

Chapter 9

How to Evaluate Your Writing

One of the most important things that you can do after you have written your first draft is to evaluate your writing. You need to make sure that your argument is clearly stated and that your writing style is clear and succinct. To help you evaluate your work, we have formulated the following checklist.

I. Evaluate Your Organization

A. **HAVE YOU WRITTEN AN INTRODUCTION THAT WILL CAPTURE AND HOLD YOUR READER'S ATTENTION?**

   1. Have you chosen a catchy "hook"?
   2. Does it lead you to ask your topic question?

B. **HAVE YOUR STATED YOUR THESIS CLEARLY AND PERSUASIVELY?**

   1. Did you find it necessary to state your topic question?
   2. Have your topic question and thesis statement been stated correctly?
   3. Have you told your reader why your topic question is important?
   4. Have you included all other relevant points?

C. HAVE YOU STRUCTURED YOUR ARGUMENT LOGICALLY?

1. Have you followed the appropriate reasoning pattern? Is your reasoning easy to follow?

2. Have you included relevant information, or did you get sidetracked? Did you spend too much time discussing collateral points?

3. Have you built a persuasive argument that tracks from paragraph to paragraph, or did you just state the main idea and fill in the rest of the essay with quotes and anecdotes?

4. Does any of your evidence look weak or inconclusive?

D. HAVE YOU WRITTEN A GOOD CONCLUSION?

Does it create an adequate sense of closure?

E. DOES YOUR TITLE ACCURATELY REFLECT THE CONTENT OF YOUR ESSAY?

II. Evaluate Your Writing

A. HAVE YOU EXPRESSED YOURSELF CLEARLY?

1. Does each of your paragraphs contain a topic sentence?

2. Is your writing crisp and interesting?

3. Are your sentences varied in length?

4. Is your subject close to the beginning of each sentence?

5. Have you refrained from using words that obscure your meaning?

B. HAVE YOU WRITTEN TOO MUCH ON SOME SUBJECTS AND TOO LITTLE ON OTHERS?

1. How do you add material if you are short?

   a. You can use a funnel paragraph or an anecdote in place of a one-sentence introduction.

   b. You can add material to the introduction as long as it does not exceed one-third the length of the final essay.

      (1) You can explore the "history of your topic."

(2) You can assess the "importance of your topic question."

c. You can add material to the discussion by:

(1) Adding additional points.

(2) Using anecdotes, illustrations, and examples.

(3) Using supplementary material that may be helpful.

d. You can expand your conclusion.

2. HOW DO YOU CUT MATERIAL IF YOUR PAPER IS TOO LONG?

a. Try putting each paragraph of your first draft in outline form. You will be amazed how superfluous words, phrases, and sentences seem to stand out. By tightening up your writing, you can avoid cutting important material.

b. In very short essays, be sure that the material in your introduction is limited to the bare essentials: opening sentence, topic question, and thesis statement.

c. Cut lengthy anecdotes and examples.

C. IS YOUR ESSAY NEATLY TYPED, PRINTED, AND SPELL-CHECKED?

1. Check for punctuation, spelling, and typing errors.

2. Check the footnotes or endnotes. Are the numbers correct? Have you followed the same format for each footnote or endnote?

a. A number of excellent guides provide information on the proper use of footnotes and endnotes. Two of the most widely used are Kate L. Turabian's *A Manual for Writers of Term Papers, Theses, and Dissertations* (The University of Chicago Press) and *MLA Handbook for Writers of Research Papers* (The Modern Language Association of America). These works also provide detailed information about the mechanics of writing, the format of research papers, and the presentation of bibliographical information.

3. Check your bibliography. Have you listed every source that you referred to in your footnotes or endnotes?

III. Congratulations! You Are Done!

Research Tips

Definition: The word *research* means to search over and over and over again.

I. Know Yourself

First of all, it is important to identify how you ordinarily go about writing and doing research. It is likely that you fit into one of these two categories:

A. **COLLECTORS:**
1. Tend to take voluminous notes in the hope that they might be useful later on.
2. Find it difficult to organize their material.
3. Tend to include material irrelevant to their argument because they spent so much time collecting it and have grown attached to it.
4. Tend to write long, disorganized, and boring essays that never seem to come to the point.

B. **WEEDERS:**
1. Tend to take selective notes directed to a specific end.
2. Tend to overlook relevant material that might enhance their argument.

3. Tend to panic when they realize they do not have enough material to fill the required number of pages. They then start to repeat themselves and to use extended quotations.

4. Tend to write short, tightly organized, and boring essays lacking in adequate proof.

C. **TAKE HEED OF YOUR OWN TENDENCIES AND TAKE STEPS TO COMPENSATE.**

II. Know What You Are Looking for

Because it is so easy to get overwhelmed by libraries, be sure that you know what kind of information you are looking for before you walk through the door. Keep your purpose in mind throughout your search.

A. ARE YOU LOOKING FOR GENERAL INFORMATION?

When you first start to do research, you are looking for general information that enables you to identify your topic question and thesis statement.

B. ARE YOU LOOKING FOR SPECIFIC INFORMATION?

After you have identified your topic question, you need to use the library to find answers to specific questions that have arisen as a result of your work. This information can be divided into four categories:

1. INFORMATION THAT BELONGS IN THE INTRODUCTION.

   a. Information that documents the importance of this topic at this time.

   b. Background information about the origin and history of the topic.

   c. Background information on any of the issues that you intend to discuss.

   d. Definitions of any confusing words or terms.

   e. Possible objections to your thesis statement.

2. FACTS THAT RELATE TO YOUR TOPIC QUESTION AND TO POINTS IN YOUR ARGUMENT.

a. You may need additional evidence to prove some of the points in your argument.

    (1) Make a note if one of your points needs further support, and try to locate additional sources of documentary evidence.

3. ANECDOTES, ILLUSTRATIONS, AND CLARIFYING EXAMPLES may be used as evidence if they support your thesis statement or points in your argument. Because they often help a subject come alive for the reader, you should try to collect a good supply of this type of evidence.

III. Know How to Take Notes

Disorganized note taking is not limited to undergraduates. We have seen Ph.D. candidates taking notes on backs of envelopes and on scraps of paper. If you work from unorganized scraps, you will most likely write an unorganized essay.

A. THE MATERIALS:

1. Use note cards because they are sturdy, portable, and sortable.

    a. 3 × 5-inch colored cards for use as bibliography cards.

    b. 4 × 6-inch white cards for research notes.

    c. 4 × 6-inch colored cards for notes to yourself, bright ideas, and questions.

2. Use letter-sized file folders for storing photocopies, drafts, and class notes.

3. Use a *pencil* to write your notes.

    a. If you do any archival work, you will not be allowed to use a pen or ballpoint.

    b. A mechanical pencil with a thin firm lead works best.

    c. Some people use a red pencil for direct quotes.

B. THE SYSTEM:

1. What goes on the bibliography card?

    a. Author's name.

b. Full title of the book.

c. Publishing house, city, year, and edition. If you are using a book with a copyright date of 1969 and an edition date of 1989, note both dates.

d. In addition, include the call number and the library where you found the reference. This saves you from having to look it up at another time.

2. What goes on the note card?

a. *Only one* note, idea, or quote per card.

b. On the back of each card, record bibliographical information in shorthand, including author, title, date of the edition, and page number.

3. Organize your cards while you are researching your project rather than waiting until the last minute.

a. Use your outline as a guide.

b. Update your outline as your research progresses.

C. AVOID USING A COMPUTER TO TAKE NOTES.

1. Computers are not easily portable and you cannot take them into some libraries.

2. Note cards, with their limited space, encourage you to *abstract* what you have read. Computers, on the other hand, encourage you to copy down long passages, a habit that is counterproductive in the long run.

D. BE CAREFUL NOT TO PLAGIARIZE MATERIAL, EVEN UNINTENTIONALLY.

1. Your difficulties begin because you are in a rush.

a. The author of the book that you are reading has a marvelous insight or has phrased an idea in such a way that you do not think that you could improve on it.

b. You take it down verbatim and vow to rewrite it later. Or maybe you just change it around a little so that you can still use that good phrase.

c. It seems too much trouble to put in those little quotation marks or to make sure that you have recorded the quote exactly or the page on which you found it.

2. By the time you sit down to organize your writing, you cannot remember what was a direct quote, what was a paraphrase, and what was your own. It all looks like your own; so you use that idea or paragraph as if it was your own.

3. Someone recognizes it and the entire value of all your work is gone in a moment. Once there is even the slightest suspicion of plagiarism, you are in trouble. If it is confirmed, you have lost a whole semester's work and maybe more.

4. Why? A careless attitude toward dishonesty in the academic community is anathema. Academic jobs depend on an honest research carefully done. It is in a teacher's interest to make sure you do careful and honest work. In the long run, it is also in your best interest.

Bibliography

Booth, Wayne C., Gregory G. Colomb and Joseph M. Williams. *The Craft of Research* (Chicago: University of Chicago Press, 1995).

Creighton, James Edwin. *An Introductory Logic,* 5th ed., rev. (New York: Macmillan, 1932).

Crews, Frederick. *The Random House Handbook,* 3d ed. (New York: Random House, 1980).

Gibaldi, Joseph and Walter S. Achtert, eds. *MLA Handbook for Writers of Research Papers* (New York: The Modern Language Association of America, 1988).

Hacker, Diana. *Rules for Writers: A Brief Handbook* (New York: St. Martin's Press, 1985).

Kelley, David. *The Art of Reasoning* (New York: W. W. Norton, 1988).

Kruger, Arthur N. *Modern Debate* (New York: 1960).

Lambeth, David. *The Golden Book on Writing* (New York: The Viking Press, 1964).

McBath, James H., ed. *Argumentation & Debate: Principles and Practice* (New York: 1960).

Rosa, Alfred and Paul Eschholz, eds. *Models for Writers* (New York: St. Martin's Press, 1982).

Stone, Wilfred H. and Robert Hoopes. *Form and Thought in Prose* (New York: The Ronald Press, 1954).

Strunk, William, Jr., and E. B. White. *The Elements of Style,* 3rd ed. (New York: Macmillan Company, 1979).

Turabian, Kate L. *A Manual for Writers of Term Papers, Theses, and Dissertations,* 5th ed. (Chicago: University of Chicago Press, 1987).

Index